FOLLOWING FLORENCE

FLORENCE

HOW I BECAME A NURSE
WHAT I'VE GOT OUT OF NURSING

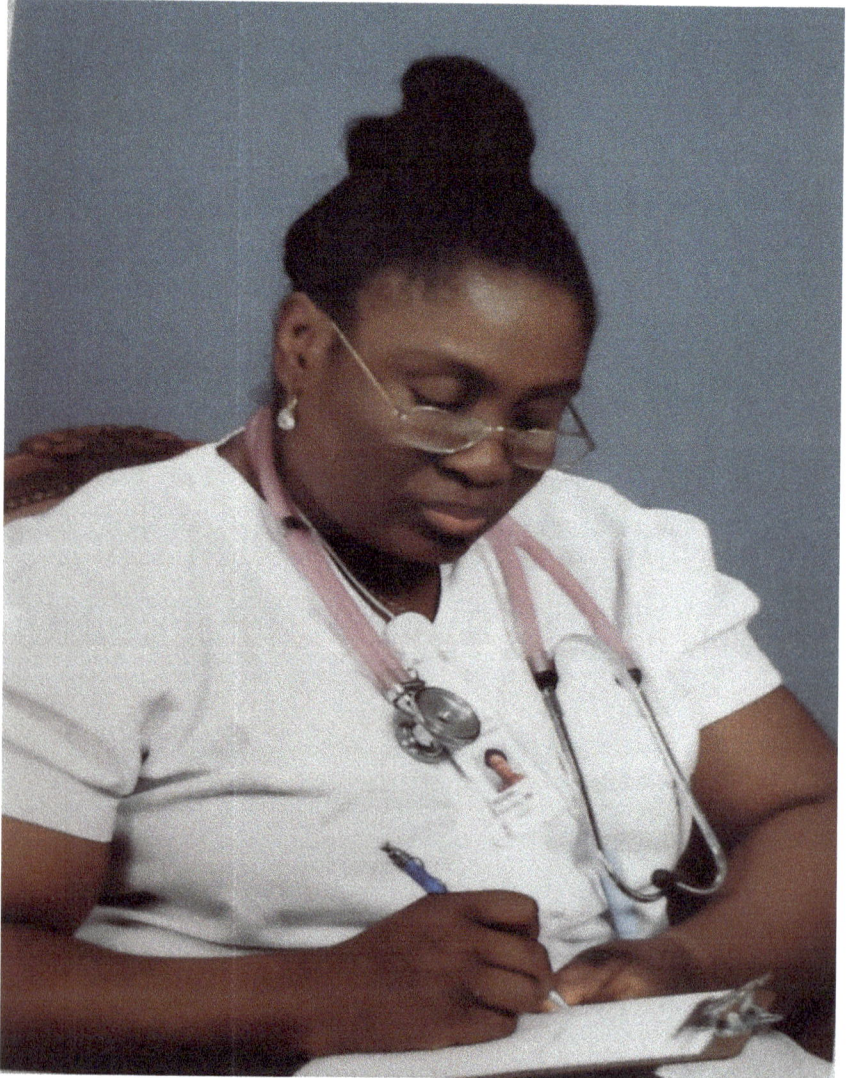

So, Child, pray say it:
Pour it out
drop
by
drop
d

r

o

p
What furnace flames have scorched your skin?
What heat has marinated your heart?
What waves have rushed your canoe?
What thirst has parched your throat?
What hunger has hollowed you out?
My tub awaits to be filled!

—the Pentina Files

FOLLOWING FLORENCE

FLORENCE

HOW I BECAME A NURSE
WHAT I'VE GOT OUT OF NURSING

Helena Martin Nagbe Franklin, RN, BSN

Following Florence
With 20 photos
Published by Pentina Publishers, Inc.

Maryland, USA
Monrovia, Liberia

© **2021 by Helena Nagbe Franklin**

ISBN: 978-0-578-24706-9

Formatted by Pen2Publishing, India

Printed at Lulu, USA

Send inquiries through
kateabela@gmail.com

This book is a Pentina Publication
under its Millennium Series.

We make cheap
Many drink deep

THIS BOOK IS DEDICATED TO

Francis W. Nagbe, I (Pa Marquis)

PAPA, YOUR CONFIDENCE
IN ME HAS ALWAYS BEEN MY STRENGTH!

Note From
The Publishers

WE AT THE PENTINA PUBLISHERS, INC. are glad to roll out the work of another exciting Liberian achiever in her very own right. The immortal Chinua Achebe set in his often referenced *Things Fall Apart*: "Looking at the mouth of a king, you will not think that he sucked at his mother's breasts." We must adapt it to the author of the present work, a wonderful soul, who came from a relatively humble beginnings to rise to her heart's desire, becoming a Professional Nurse. We take significant interest in those Liberians and other similarly situated who do have a story that is much inspiring but could go unnoticed and unheard, absent the well-deserving platform.

One crucial theme in this work is Helena's wrestle with understanding occurrences in both the visible and invisible worlds. It is a relevant question which people throughout the ages have confronted. The grappling is part of what makes life dynamic with its daunting and yet delightful chapters. It is one great theme of life that requires a never-ending conversation. It is a theme that inevitably draws to us the need to not take for granted information and people we all meet from time to time.

But Helena's story is more than grappling with occurrences in both the visible and invisible worlds. In this debuting author's work, we experience, even if vicariously, the intrigues of war—from enjoying the benefits of professional competency, to weaseling out of potential dangers driven by reckless rebels who with their guns feel entitled to take to their groin every woman they meet and just anything of perceived value they lay eyes on.

Helena's strategy of meeting some of the risks that she experienced during the Liberian civil war without losing her cool, and her showing that "soft words turn away wrath" will help make *Following Florence* a beautiful read. In one of her stories where a woman gradually treks through subtle domestic violence until she hits the wall of emotional wreckage, literally going out of her mind, we watch Helena getting to work and bringing the woman around to the joy and reassurance of life. Helena's professional service here is not one of gloating about kindness or professional proficiency but one of showing how care and concern can help shape a world in which insensitivity abounds and can do significant destruction. This is also true when she talks about a patient who goes home with a nasogastric tube, his family not fully educated about how to manage him in homecare settings. And how about a woman who craves for relief from a foreign object left inside of her after a C-section operation, but never gets the deserving attention!

Utility of the Book

Following Florence is deceptively short. Sometimes, the power of a book is not in the length but in the energy it exudes. *Following Florence* is packed with a variety of emotions and lessons that will keep the heart warm and challenge readers to perform daily acts that give the vulnerable of the world reasons to hope for attention and deserving care.

It needs to be said that *Following Florence* may be useable in more serious ways than one. In chapters 1, 2, 4, and 5, for example, readers will learn that people should be open to multiple layers of truth—as it relates mainly to realities of the visible and invisible forces and voices in the world. Given people's prior individual perceptions and predispositions, it may be humanly possible sometimes to hedge on the acceptance of "new truths". Nonetheless, creating and sustaining the curiosity of pursuing each layer of truth to its possible logical end infuses the capacity of one to believe in the importance of human collaboration and possibilities of progress.

In chapters 2 and 3, the book shows that when faced with a moment of crisis, staying calm and hopeful is preferable. That way, you can quietly sort out appropriate words and actions that may likely lead to refreshing results. After all, a cool head provides an opportunity for useful thinking that processes as many aspects of the consequences as possible, and hopefully leads to choosing very rewarding consequences. This lesson applies not only to the health industry but also to life in general. It worked for Helena in her wartime years. If keeping composed "under fire" doesn't serve well, the consolation will then be that at least you did try to do the humanly proper thing.

Chapters 5, 6, and 8 speak to the reality that any situation or condition may likely escalate to a critical, physical or mental harm that may demand an unusual volume of resources or may become irreversible. Thus, the need to act often with urgency or to keep proactive strategies in the arsenal of resolving or managing problems, if not conflicts, is often the best way to go in pursuing matters of administration or management. This should be true in all fields of discipline.

Another point to the useful aspects of Helena's book, as set in chapter 5, is the implicit introduction of the legal theme of sources of evidence. In the matters of jurisprudence, gathering evidence to indict a potential culprit can be head-spinning and hair-splitting, indeed, downright frustrating. Sometimes the unwanted need for plea-bargaining may be the painful option. Plea bargaining is a judicial concept evoked in a case. It helps to somewhat resolve a case when the possibility of resolving the case is fraught with challenges that cannot be removed absent the confession of the presumed culprit or some witness to a crime. Plea bargaining usually leads to less intense punitive actions.

In Helena's book, when a young man who deals in Indian mysticism is likely to add to his list of escapades the impactful theft of a steel safe packed with a whole institution's funds for operation and salaries, the ordinary Anglo-American methods of gathering evidence—searching for the words of the potential culprit, the possible tools or weapons of the crime, monitoring of actions to establish intent and motive, etc.—cannot serve the police. Fortunately, an extra judicial method in Anglo-American law becomes willy-nilly acceptable. An African Customary law tool of evidence-gathering becomes useful. The rituals of a fetish priest become the inevitable path to solving the case. This situation even brings in an aspect of philosophy—utilitarian ethics. This has to do with the considering of a good act as the act which brings about the greatest good for the greatest number of people. John Stuart Mills' and Jeremy Bentham's thoughts on utilitarian ethics are relevant in the implicit thought process of the fetish priest who helps solve the mystery of the theft, even when he knows that he will die shortly thereafter because of the help he provides. His decision to act, being fully aware of the personal consequences, is additionally a matter of existentialism—knowing and owning to the consequences one's actions.

In chapter 8 of Helena's book also lies the thought on cultural literacy where a health care giver is often urged to seek the understanding of patients' cultural perceptions, behaviors, and attitudes in order to offer the appropriate advice regarding the appropriate regimen of treatments. Additionally, Helena's book evokes the subject of the need for health care givers to respect patients' right to autonomy—the ability to respect each patient's right of independence to the person and to the slew of possible medications and procedures. But what if a specific, potential patient decides to pursue what seems therapeutic actions that have the potential of exacerbating the health problem? The book suggests that in such a scenario, the health care giver needs to take up the duty of beneficence, remembering that driven by training, knowledge, and skills, all health care givers must provide the appropriate guidance to better healing protocols. When a man who has contracted Hepatitis or "yellow jaundice" refuses to seek a cure using Western medicine, and instead he begins to apply alternative medicine by consuming snake soup, Helena steps in. Eventually, the man and his wife have Helena to thank.

In essence, if a book is as useful as the variety of lessons it can provide, then Helena's *Following Florence* is really up to the task. So, again, this book has numerous lessons that should inspire readers to perform daily acts that give the vulnerable of the world reasons to hope for attention and deserving care. If that is done, Mrs. Helena Franklin's effort would have been well-rewarded.

We ask for a strong public support to advance any meaningful program or project that this beautiful soul—who overcame adversity to achieve her dream of becoming a Professional Nurse—would like to undertake.

The Pentina Publishers
Maryland, USA
February 2021

The Author's Note

I GREW UP AND LATER WORKED in rural Liberia. Liberia is in the company of three West African countries, including Sierra Leone, Guinea, and the Ivory Coast. In that Liberia I experienced so many interesting and intriguing things. And as the years passed, I began to reflect on these things with many friends and acquaintances. In the end, I thought it was time to share some of the stories with a broader audience. You will therefore understand that even though I have my health professional audience in mind, this book speaks to a much wider audience. In light of that, I've tried to use a language that is not all too intimidating. I've used comparatively lesser professional jargon.

xviii   Following Florence

The health profession, which I gradually grew fond of, became an important gateway. The health profession is massive, massive in terms of huge populations of people to engage with, massive in terms of materials to work with. One never knows the reality until one is initiated into it. So many things I encountered, so many people I encountered, so many health problems many colleagues and I dealt with when I was at a relatively young age. How these problems were navigated and resolved might make awesome reading. Therefore, I have decided to share a significant portion of my experiences with you, my audience, with the hope that someone somewhere may be entertained, enlightened, or inspired to work in ways to bring relief to people around the world. The result is this short work—*Following Florence: How I Became a Nurse and What I've Got Out of Nursing.* As most people familiar with the history of Nursing know, Florence refers to Florence Nightingale, the Mother of the Nursing profession. Besides, in an era where the Corona pandemic has brought the significance of the health industry into strong and wider public view, who would not want to hear or read back stories of nurses and doctors—these members of an essential sector of society, and what infuses them with much energy in their strife to help bring care and comfort to people everywhere and in varied circumstances?

A few initial experiences sparked my interest in the healthcare industry. The first happened to be about a little child's enthusiasm to help hand medications to parents and grandparents at home. The second happened to have been about a near death experience of a teenage mother in a public hospital where the odds of receiving critical care seemed non-existent. The very inspiring reassurance of the profession that for everyone, there is "the right to adequate, quality, and timely care despite the age, social status, creed, etc." seemed too distant. Additionally, the assertion that "all patients deserve to be treated equally and with compassion at all times by [each] health care team" seemed applicable only on a different planet.

As a child, I often admired nurses in their sparkling white uniforms, their stethoscopes, and other accessories swinging from them. My passion for the profession would grow immensely beyond such superficial basics. It would become very compelling. I always felt a personal gratification watching the air of comfort, relief, and smiles wash over my sick siblings, my grandfather, and so on, while continuing care for them on their sick beds at home, following physicians' instructions after inpatient and or outpatient visits at different times. Often, the clinician-guided care included the giving of medications, the providing of what seemed tasteful meals to boost the patients' appetite and restore the needed energy levels. The patients were kept clean and comfortable. They were monitored to ensure that their basic needs were met in order to speed up an anticipated and well-deserved recovery. Attending to these patients with compassion at the higher level, I'd hoped, would be a no-brainer as I fantasized about what I would do if I became a nurse. Sadly, several years later when I became a teen mother, the bitter taste of child delivery somewhat disabused me of that fantasy. I was entering high school, then. Lying in a hospital bed, sick, helpless, and compromised, with my first born out of my womb, I could not believe that I would be treated to a serious neglect that nearly cost me my life. That neglect did happen—Good Lord, it did!

WHEN THE MOMENT CAME to deliver, I found myself in a public hospital. There, except for God's possible presence and the intervention of an older patient who and I shared the ward, it would have been a different story. In the strongest voice, she directed the nursing staff, who had brought in breakfast, to first attend to me: "You must attend to this girl before attending to me because her voice is getting weaker and weaker as she continues to call for help, and you all keep ignoring her!"

At the moment, the woman's voice sounded like she was so far away from me. I could barely open my eyes. It seemed that she was well known and respected by the staff. A multigravida, whose steps had beaten the path to the hospital for the delivery of her seven children, she was significantly known. After all, I'd learn later that she was well at home with the staff. She'd often offered gratuities which, no doubt, earned her a place in the hospital where her requests returned with purpose and meaning. Obviously, the fact that the culture of gratuities in the hospital environment was often discouraged had no audience here. Perhaps, had the converse of refusing gratuities been true, how would I have been the beneficiary of her generosity! Who can easily understand which flicker of light can shine through the darkest clouds of life!

The experience must be one of my early teary moments. I was having postpartum hemorrhage. This meant I was incurring heavy bleeding that would not slow or stop. There was a drop in my blood pressure. This was accompanied by a blurry vision. I was experiencing chills and clammy skin. In this condition, any number of other signs and symptoms shuttled in and out—fast heartbeat, getting confused, dizzy, sleepy, or weak, or feeling a sense of fainting, and feeling nausea.

I'd had prolonged labor, and then a full bladder. I gave birth to a male child on April 26, 1975, between 9pm and 10pm, which was during the second shift at the hospital. However, I was never attended to by the care team from the moment I was taken to my bed from the delivery room. The bleeding noticeably subsided gradually during the first shift of the next day, which was April 27, 1975—thanks to the intervention of a midwife who helped me empty my bladder.

I remember she screened my bed to provide privacy, put me on a bedpan, slightly raised the head of the bed, and I felt her pouring warm water on my lower abdomen. This helped me empty my bladder. I felt much relief even though the bleeding didn't slow nor stop immediately. At last, the kind woman washed me up and provided me a fresh clean gown. She brought me breakfast and monitored my progress consistently. In life, when much sought relief arrives, nothing else easily explains the doors to heaven! The woman provided emotional support, keeping me as calm as possible. During her shift, she applied all appropriate interventions and the bleeding slowed to normal. When I felt a lot improved and more alert, I saw an IV hanging over me and infusing. I asked why an IV? The midwife told me that seemingly I was going into shock. My blood pressure, she said further, was so low that it couldn't be read accurately, and that the rest of my vital signs were also very unstable. My knowledge regarding the cause of postpartum hemorrhage would expand during my study in nursing school, specifically when I took classes in Obstetrics and Gynecology (OB/GYN).

Before the end of the second shift, on that April 26th day, I bled excessively and began to feel weak. My bladder was very full, and I needed help to use the toilet or a bedpan. No staff hand would come around to assist me despite my many calls for help. Nurse aides continued to give such excuses as, "I'll be back, I'm very busy." During shift change, as the second and third shifts midwives conducted their bedside report from room to room, I requested for help. Someone promised to return. After some-time, she returned with a bedpan and helped to get me on it. I was very uncomfortable and could not bear to use it due to the biting pain I was feel-ing. I explained my condition to the available nurse aide. I told her to pass that information on to a midwife; I needed relief for my grave discom-fort. She agreed. It turned out that it was an empty response. I neither got any medication nor got any help to empty my bladder. Looking back today at the whole phenomenon of birth pain, I can under-stand why when a child offends a mother, espe-cially in a very serious way, she easily offers deep regrets. Yet, mothers that are reflective are mothers that keep a healthy mind and soul.

Anyway, the day shift came in. At about breakfast time, an aide came in to change my beddings. I asked her to help me to the bathroom because I was so weak and couldn't help myself. She told me to transfer into a chair at the bedside. Just as I was attempting to get up from the bed, I felt very weak and very dizzy, feeling faint and wanted a hand to hold onto. Without offering a hand, the woman said, "Help yourself-o. I just here to make up your bed." In Liberia, as you will keep in mind, our local type of English, call it Liberian Pidgin, carries the extra "o" as some extension. That aspect is very distinctive. I pleaded with the woman to help me because I was feeling too weak and dizzy to stand and turn around. I told her the entire room was spinning, and I was feeling too dizzy. At this point, one of my roommates called for someone. It must have been either a nurse or a midwife.

Little did I know that my advocate was a blood relative. Everything unfolded when my mother walked in to visit me that afternoon. Both were so happy to see each other. "What are you doing here?"

she said to my mother. "Here to see my daughter," Mom answered. And then Mom introduced me to her. Obviously, she hadn't seen me, although she had heard about me. From that moment onwards, you can guess the kind of care I got from the hospital staff until I was discharged. My "aunty" (as I started referring to the woman) spent a few more days because she had a tubal ligation, a fancy phrase for the surgical procedure whereby a woman's fallopian tubes are tied to prevent pregnancy.

Needless to say, my rite of passage into motherhood with all its signals of what is often referred to as connection power—the well-known "who knows you" culture in the world—has never easily left me. But to be honest, what has not left me from that past experience is that disengaged health care service simply has to be no service at all! One will understand why throughout my professional journey I have tried, as much as humanly possible, to sustain a sense of reassurance and to keep hope alive among those that I serve or interact with.

I close with great thanks to the Pentina Group, this Liberian group, for providing me an important platform. Nudging me, probing me, they helped strengthen in me a storytelling talent that seemed to have been asleep. Working with the team, I learned so much, both about myself and about the writing process. It was quite a humbling experience.

So, here I start this initial part of my life story, hoping you find it interesting. Every adult life is a web of so many other lives. Therefore, such an adult cannot tell a personal story without other names, voices, and places coming in. You will obviously understand why every now and then I will use slightly different names and places. The people, especially, didn't possibly ask for this exposure. It must be kept in mind, though, that every strand of this life story I tell in here is very true. So, be warmed, be touched, be inspired—if possible!

Helena Martin Nagbe Franklin, RN, BSN
Reynoldsburg, Ohio
February 2021

Acknowledgements

For my life, my engagements, and my productivity, I do recognize and thank so many people. Here is a representative list:

- *David K. Franklin, Sr*
  My husband, you understand the importance/challenges of us being one, yet separate beings with different thoughts, dreams, and views. Your understanding and acceptance signify a great deal of respect, giving me new strength each day and overcoming fear. A great educator!

- *My Children and Grandchildren*
  Your **LOVE** inspires me.

- *Valarie Franklin ('My Queen")*
  An integral part of my First Responders—one I won't trade for anything!

- *Rev. Peter Nehsahn. Borcon Jue. Wilma Kpohanu. Linda Gaba Richards* Very lovely minds and hearts—Where would my family have been without you! I do give God the glory for you!

- *K-Moses Nagbe, PhD*
  Your words of wisdom and encouragement planted the seed of this empowering project.

- *Rev. Fr. Thomas Hayden*
  You contributed immensely to the walls of my education, ensuring that I achieved my desired career.

- *Rev. Sr. Mary Rose Heery*
  You've been a great motivator who always sees the good in others.

- *Loretta Gruver*
  You were my hero. My greatest dream is to become a Professional Nurse as you and other nursing educators molded me to be.

- *To the Women of Good Breeding*
  [Sophie T. Parwon, Jane A. Samukai, Ellen M. Gbanlon, and Comfort Y. Flemming]
  I am forever grateful to the angel that brought our paths together.

Table Of Contents

CHAPTER ONE

Early Schooling and My Path to Nursing

MY LIFE BEGAN IN SASSTOWN, RURAL Liberia—southeast of the country—West Africa. Sasstown is a home of people tough-minded, but generous of spirit. When I think about my birth, I think about a childhood friend of mine. He has often spoken and even written about the diversity of individual personalities, personalities for which we need not crawl about frantically to offer apologies or drive ourselves sick concerning how, when, where, or why we were individually born. He has often said: "Breaking sweat over decisions regarding the prenatal configuration of your life is something next to insanity. As far as cognitive abilities go, you were not there at the moment of

1

that configuration. Just at your natal emergence into the world, simply brace yourself to begin your very own life. So the Supreme deals, so you abide, period." Furthermore, in "The Walking Conundrum Finds Healing," he writes:

> Perhaps, that's what it's all about:
> To accept the inevitable
> And make it as palatable as possible.
> By that, scale back on dark energies
> That rot rather than revive
> Smother rather than save—
> Life without tantrums
> Is life triumphant.

My life began as the child of two young adults growing up in the same community. Being students and in a rural setting, their parents obviously wished for a different outcome. Accordingly, both youthful parents left town, one after the other. But I really grew significantly in the shadow of my maternal family, especially my maternal grandparents. I would feel the presence of my dad when in my teens, carrying a baby and yet craving for an education, I traveled to Monrovia where both parents had separately gone. Overtime, I grew to love and appreciate both of them. But my mother and my maternal grandparents! They were souls out of the world!

Very many years later, on May 10, 2020, I would celebrate Mom, whom I grew fondly to reference as *Cici*, which is funny because this is a fond name all young people give to middle-aged women in my childhood community. Much older women have been referenced as Mama. There doesn't have to be any biological relationship. I don't know how the name Cici stuck with me, but I think by the time we came permanently into each other's company, I was relatively old enough and a Momma reference did not seem age appropriate.

Anyway, when I along with my younger siblings celebrated her, I, being the eldest of the children, took the local traditional path of adulation. I reeled off her names—Theresa Wiah Gbei-Sunday, Gbesi Nagbe Wiah Gbei, Nimene Wèllèh Gbei; *À Dì (ah dee), Jobodì, Jowlo,* Mama!

Her natural and fond names having been lined up, I went on to thank her for what she'd been in our lives. She had been a very quiet and calm heroine whose virtues mainly of patience and working hard sustained us. Her love and kindness have remained beyond description. Life tried so hard to give her hundreds of reasons to cry, but she often told us that there were countless reasons to smile, to laugh, to dance, looking at the generations that came into this world through her, the only daughter of a woman who did not have a chance to bask in motherhood.

By the time we celebrated Cici, "her vase," as locals often say, "had produced a whole village." After all, for the rural mind the more the working hands in a household, the more well-settled the home is. Cici had produced eleven children, with two dead; twenty-nine grandchildren; and twenty great grandchildren. Her mother would have possibly laughed, or perhaps sighed with relief, saying: "Well, Child, I won't blame you. I left you so early, you alone. You possibly had to carry the rest of the feminine fruits I couldn't bear before I left the world."

Cici was indeed the lone child of twenty-eight-year-old Toyà Nimene Wèllèh, her mother, who departed this world when Cici was eight years old. The little girl ended up carrying some fuzzy memory of the mother. For most of those eight years, the mother was very ill and often for months on end, she was away from home. Usually, she was taken to the farthest point of rural Liberia, east of Sasstown, to the J. J. Dossen Hospital in Harper, Maryland County, one of several counties in the country. She would undergo a number of surgeries. At other times, she was treated with alternative medications—mainly herbal treatment. Eventually, she succumbed to the strange abdominal ailment.

Well, Cici was left with the father and his second wife who proved loving to Cici, to me, and to the rest of Cici's children that she had by Peter Sunday who eventually became my stepfather. He would die by the time we celebrated our dear mother in 2010. Cici's father, Grandpa, proved equally loving. He also was very industrious. He kept a considerable number of livestock and was one of the few prosperous local shop-owners. Eventually, he served as the local postmaster, a position that gave him even greater clout in the community. The fact is that through him numerous rural residents heard from several satellite cities and of course from Monrovia, the big city. Doubtless, he could not be an ordinary person. By Grandpa's second wife, he produced five children, bringing all his children to the total of six, with Cici being the third and only daughter in the brood. Today, all her brothers have passed. Today, Grandpa, Francis Wiah Nagbe, I, too, has passed.

The phenomenon of his death and other phenomena later in my life have left me cognizant and respectful of occurrences in both the visible and the invisible worlds of life. These experiences continue to help me see science, as it is generally known, not as the be all and the end all of things. The concept of science insists upon evidence that should be accessed through all five human senses; that the experimental path to the evidence should be so clear that anybody other than the original experimenter should be able to come up with the evidence as exact or near exact as the original evidence. It turns out then that science, as it is generally known, speaks to what just anybody can see, touch, hear, taste, and smell. This reasoning is sometimes set in the well-known phrase of "evidence-based" practices. According to this presumed "objective reality," any circumstance or situation beyond that phase of occurrences should be characterized as non-existent or simply false, absurd, or superstitious. As it relates to natural occurrences, it would seem to me that truth or fact as an apparent monolithic concept must be treated with some significant degree of caution.

Sometime ago, I learned of two relatable and insightful incidents. First, I learned that President Abraham Lincoln of America dreamed of his own death in a night prior to the real assassination of the revered president in a Washington, D. C. theatre—Ford's Theatre. He was shot there and died the following day, April 14, 1865. How could his dream and his death have been so aligned in a disconcerting way?

The second incident was about a haunted home. A priest spoke to the need for caution in such matters as pertain to the concept of truth. I learned that he wrote the preface to a book titled *The Amityville Horror*. It was a book cataloguing the experiences of a couple that moved into a haunted home in a village called Amityville. I understand that Amityville is in a town called Babylon in Suffolk County in New York state, the United States of America. Any normal person would have seriously doubted that couple's experiences—e.g., hearing footsteps around but seeing nobody; hearing voices but seeing no utterers of the voices; seeing or hearing furniture falling or crashing; feeling extremely cold in spite of a heated home; etc.

However, the priest, who also had been drawn into that whirlpool of experiences because he had been initially called in to bless the home, wrote that people need to provide a space in their minds for religion, science, and the otherworldly—superstition. Each, he explained, is contributory to the full circle of truth and must be respected. In other words, the world is made of both the visible and the invisible. Anyone doubting this concept of the world simply needs to think again. Thus, studies in mysticism, parapsychology, paranormal, telepathy, etc. should have their place in life with all their multi-layered complexities. In other words, let us not be totally dismissive of information simply because we think "it does not make sense." Sometimes readily regarding something as making no sense is showing a weak capacity for rigorous thinking. We probably need to take information in and begin to explore all facets that relate to it. Of course, exploration does not have to be an instant process.

Doubtless, prior to the foregoing experiences I listed and the knowledge gained, my grandfather's death would have shaken something inside of me about life, just as something about life would shake inside of me when I graduated from a middle level nursing program at the Winifred J. Harley United Methodist School of Nursing and began to work at a prominent community clinic. Life, surely, is replete with numerous complexities beyond human comprehension. The incident that occurred while I was working at the clinic, I will discuss much later in Chapter Five about how Fred, a young man steeped in India mysticism, would have outwitted a whole despairing community, had an old fetish priest not blocked his intrigues and escapades.

But let me now talk about the incident with Grandpa. You see, when human minds bond, there's no telling what may run between and amongst those minds. The phenomena of telepathy and paranormality can be relevant here. To say that my maternal grandfather loved me is to really make an understatement. Growing up with him, I felt there was nothing humanly possible he would ever fail to do for me. For this reason, when I strayed off course momentarily in my teen years, I felt I had disappointed him. Yet, I was his *Tarpèduh,* a fond name he rarely skipped.

The year he passed was 1981. I had completed high school and enrolled at W. J. Harley for my nursing training. Earlier that year, passing through Ganta, a mid-country city, he stopped on my campus. We hadn't seen each other for a long while, so the visit was a refreshing reunion. I guess his *Tarpèduh,* back on track and racing to make something of her life filled up his mind. Joy was palpable in his face, in his eyes. One of my maternal uncles had fallen on bad times; he was being taken to Monrovia to work on his mental health, which was a problem in its early stages.

Sr. Ann Justin, one of the few nuns operating a little Catholic clinic in Sasstown, had accepted to take Grandpa and my uncle to Monrovia. As they explained that day, they got on the school campus and met Ms. Loretta Gruver, the Director of Nursing, and told her that they were on campus to see one of the nursing students, Helena. That was how I was fetched from class.

Sr. Ann Justin was really a household name back in Sasstown. I did remember her. It was she who treated a chronic neck pain I often had. Eventually, she recommended that I went to Harper, Maryland, to get further treatment at J. J. Dossen Hospital, yes, the same hospital that my maternal grandmother attended very many years earlier. I traveled by a motorized canoe, one of those owned by the Fanti cultural group that migrated from Ghana many years earlier and have become a solid part of the Liberian society. When my treatment was over, I returned by an airplane operated by the Catholic Mission. Fr. Benedict Dotu Sekey was one of the pilots. He flew me back after about two or three weeks of treatment. It turned out I had chronic tonsillitis. The trip was around 1972.

Anyway, Sr. Ann Justin, Grandpa, and my uncle resumed their journey from the W. J. Harley campus to Monrovia. My uncle was admitted to the Catherine Mills Rehabilitation Center. Grandpa, too, having gotten ill, was admitted at the ELWA Hospital. This is a protestant-evangelical hospital. Grandpa remained there for about three weeks, became an outpatient for about another week, and then flew back to Sasstown.

In the latter part of the year, it was final exams for the junior year, which was the second of the three years I expected to spend in that school. The night prior to taking the last of my exams, I and my roommate sat studying by a window. Our dormitories were bungalows. You could sit in bed and, if close by any of the several trees decking the campus, see what was going on under the tree. There were a few large trees standing at the back of my dormitory. In the day, we would sit in the shades of the trees.

That night of the eve of the exam was unusually quiet. Every now and then, some theme of conversation would come up and my roommate and I would eat it up. In the midst of that, between 9 and 12, I heard from the direction of the trees nearby what seemed Grandpa's voice: "*Tarpèduh. Tarpèduh. Nyonoh Wlè Plee.*" The voice was deliberate. It was delightful. It was wonderful. Yet, it was shocking. Where was Grandpa coming from or going at the time of the night? If only there had been cellphones in those days!

I called my friend's attention to it: "I heard someone call me right now—like my grandfather."

"Uh, Helena. Maybe you're hallucinating," Ellen said.

"Not joking."

"Okay—."

Silence.

I quietly reflected on what I thought had just happened. When it came time to call it a night, we did. I went to sleep. After some time, I began to have a dream. In the dream, my dear grandfather, people knew as Pa Marquis, was lying in a casket surrounded by mourners. The dream was so intense that visiting the bathroom and returning to resume my sleep did not cut off a bit of the story. The dream returned.

In the morning, I was racked by anxiety. I told Ellen about the dream. Ellen resumed the themes of hallucination and matters related to the subconscious. She said that the dream was probably triggered by the conversation we had the previous night.

Luckily, it was on a Friday. After the exam, I was scheduled to take a quick trip to Monrovia to get a gift for the lone student who was graduating that year. I would take some of that time to visit my mom before returning to Ganta in the evening. So, I left Ganta. I arrived in Monrovia, and as usual went to Mom's home. There, I came to the horrible, obnoxious, jaw-dropping reality—Francis Wiah Nagbe, I, Gbisi Nagbe Wiah, Pa Marquis, *Wli nè mø nyøn* [Money Is One's True Relation], my loving grandfather whom I saw in the casket in my dream was really dead. He'd died the previous night. The voice the previous night was probably part of the mysterious energy which ordinary humans cannot understand. Grandpa came perhaps to bid Granddaughter farewell. The mysteries of life will never end!

The explanation about his death was that in the morning, back in Sasstown, he got up and swept the yard as he often did. Meantime, his water was on the fire. That's the rural land—people heat their water in pots on the fire hearth. When the water is hot enough, it is poured into a bucket and taken to an outfence built of bamboo reed or palm frond. In his case, the younger sister of his previously dead wife, Toyà Nimene Wèllèh, had come around that morning as she usually did. Toyà Nimene Tàlor, this younger, former sister-in-law, was on her way to her farm, a few miles away. In rural lands, a farm serves several purposes. One of them is a "grocery store" where inhabitants go to harvest pepper, greens, eggplants, mushrooms, palm nuts, and a few other edibles for two or three-day meals. So, except for Sunday, the farm road often becomes a thoroughfare.

While Grandpa was completing the sweeping chore, Nimene Tàlor, who considered herself a solid part of the home, got the old man's water ready. He now went into his room to get his towel and soap. He was in there for extra, unusual minutes. When the woman went to check up on him, he was lying across his bed, dead. Did he have a heart attack? Just what had happened?

Well, sadly that was it. The old man died. Today, my mother's father, her stepmother, and her brothers have all passed. And at 79, she's returned to the situation of filial lonesomeness—except, of course, she has her children and grandchildren to somewhat keep her company.

How about Ellen? She was floored when she learned that Grandpa died. She couldn't believe that "my head was that straight"!—a local way of saying my dreams were simply too frighteningly real for comfort. And perhaps too weird? Just how was it possible that someone would have such a dream and almost minute-by-minute all its parts would fall into place in reality? Ellen did grieve with me. My hope was that eventually like me, she would understand that life has so many mysteries that human beings can never fully understand, and that the best thing to do always is to keep an open mind.

SO, YES. MY LIFE began in Sasstown, Grand Kru County, Liberia, West Africa. There I began my elementary school with my grandparents. My mother, as I said earlier, had long moved to Monrovia, Liberia's capital city. She'd make a few intermittent visits back to Sasstown. By the time I was completing my middle school years, I found myself pregnant—who can sometimes know the ways of adolescents! I therefore moved to my mother. No sooner had I moved there than I entered a nearby public school, the Boatswain Junior High School. I attended that school up to and after the delivery of my little boy that I have already spoken about. It was really in my last days of ninth grade; Liberia treats ninth grade as the last year in junior high or middle school. When my middle school days were done, I continued to be fired up for an education. That was how I entered the Monrovia College and Industrial Training School. This was a high school with a vocational curriculum, as the name indicates. I did complete my course work in 1979.

With that done, I began to think seriously about becoming a professional nurse. I must confess here, though, that becoming a nurse had taken a few other possible dreams into company. At one point, for example, I wanted to become an office secretary because I'd acquired secretarial skills in high school. The only reason for that dream was that I admired females behind desks with individual typewriters and performing clerical duties. At another point, I dreamed to become an accounts manager to work for a big business company, and then subsequently establish my own business to earn more money. I derived this desire from observing Grandpa back in Sasstown and Mother in Monrovia as she steered her own wheel of a quasi-thrifty shop (i.e., a used clothes business). Being inexperienced and trying to complete high school, I had my own doubts about the job market and could not imagine how quickly I could achieve such a dream of a self-owned business within a reasonable time. Yet, the desire for nursing trumped it all.

So, hearing about a school in another rural region, north of the country, I braced myself to apply. It was the Winifred J. Harley United Methodist School of Nursing, which offered a rigorous, three-year registered nursing program. I would take this professional journey from February 1980 to December 1982.

If only a journey were as smooth as what a few words on paper made it sound and seem! Prior to enrolling into W.J. Harley, I went through a very tough screening which was a tougher and final phase of screening to qualify candidates. Comparatively, the entrance examination was a no-brainer. The later intense cross examination nearly flung me out of the process. The interview team included seven members comprising clinical administrators, junior staff members, and a few instructors. I still remember the day they called me into the room of deliberation, seated in a semi-circle. Some sat stone-faced, one or two smiling. Soon, the questions began. To date, some of these questions refuse to leave my mind:

ONE: "Why do you want to do Nursing?" This was followed up with an explanatory comment: "Nurses are not making decent salaries to meet their needs. Do you still want to pursue Nursing?"

At that level of my education, I sensed by intuition that such a question would be in the midst of myriad questions. I told the team that I wanted to study and practice as a nurse because of the personal satisfaction I continued to enjoy from helping others and my desire to be an advocate for the neglected and abused in society. This answer was at my fingertips because I asked myself a dozen times before I even took the entrance exam.

TWO: "If a patient with leprosy stretches forth his/her hand for a handshake, will you shake the hand?"

I agreed I would, because it would be my duty as a nurse to make my patients feel accepted and assured that I would perform my duties without reservation—except otherwise cautioned about when to avoid physical contact with patients due to certain diseases or viruses.

If I thought I had pulled through, it was not so fast. My physical examination showed traces of hypertension. Beneath all that tension of engaging with the school administrators was an elevated level of anxiety. Psychologists remind us that sometimes the questioning of our own abilities induces fear that easily affects our performances, highlighting some self-fulling prophecy. I had no prior history of hypertension. In any case, I was told to go home for the day and return for a follow up after one week. I complied. When I returned, my vital signs returned to normal and the admission process sailed to the end. Gladly, I became a bona fide student at the school.

Thus, I became an added number to what was a sprawling community known as the Ganta United Methodist Mission. The Mission comprised of a high school, a pastoral center that doubled as a modest pastoral school for in-service training of pastors, a hospital, the nursing school, and a relaxation park. There was also an airstrip. My section of the Mission, the W. J. Harley School of Nursing, had dormitories for students. In the first year, it was mandatory to live on campus. After that, students were at liberty to either live on campus or commute. Living on campus was free. At W. J. Harley, we had three meals daily from a mess hall. However, each dormitory had a kitchen fitted with facilities for private meals. Life had its ups and downs, but W. J. Harley was equally an exciting place to be.

There was another point which would be settled clearly in my first year. During the interview phase to my acceptance, I had been perceived as "unapproachable," something which meant that my patients and my colleagues would be intimidated by my presence. The issue was debated and subsequently resolved in my favor. I got to know about that intra-team conversation during my training. One of the clinical instructors intimated that incident as she completed my first performance evaluation in my freshman year. She was very impressed by my performance relating, first, to student nurse and patient relationship, and, second, to my good rapport with my senior staff and my colleagues. At the end of my freshman year, I was voted as the Most Sociable by the school newspaper.

From that point onwards, the weeks came and went; the months came and went, the years came and went. As the end of my last, that is the third, year approached, I began to prepare for my psychiatry practicum or "Psyc Affiliation," as we often called it. This practicum would be done at the Catherine Mills Rehabilitation Center, the public mental health institution where my maternal uncle had sought treatment.

Naturally, it was time also to begin planning to rise to the next level of my life. I began to send out feelers for a job. One such place was the Catholic Secretariat in the Archdiocese of Monrovia. You see, being a Catholic, my very path to W. J. Harley had, in some respects, been paved by some volunteering work I had done in my parish. While in high school, I had taken interest in helping to care for the floral plants in the church compound. That was how to my delight I was, one day, informed about possible scholarships to attend the nursing school. Thus, volunteering work does have some surprising rewards.

Nearing my completion of W. J. Harley, I thought to seek a position as a staff nurse with the major Catholic hospital in Monrovia or with any other affiliate institution. I had earlier spoken to Rev. Sr. Dr. Margaret Chambers, MD, about the plan. I had often related to her as my advisor/counselor while a student at W. J. Harley, the school which I was now completing. Dr. Chambers then was the Medical Director of the Ganta Leprosy Colony, Nimba County. She recommended me to Archbishop Michael K. Francis, a once towering cleric in the Catholic Church of Liberia. To imagine that this great soul has now passed!

On a bright Monday morning, at the Catherine Mills Rehabilitation Center, while we (nursing students) were in the dining hall for breakfast, I saw three Catholic nuns come up the stairs. They stood at the dining entrance. I walked out to greet and ask if they needed help. They introduced themselves as Rev. Sr. Rita, Rev. Sr. Isabel, and Rev. Sr. Paula. Sr. Rita said they were out at W. J. Harley to meet student Helena Nagbe. "But we do not know her in person."

Without hesitation and without knowing their mission, I revealed immediately that I was the one

being sought. In the environment of the familiar, how could I have entertained any doubts! Sr.
Rita hugged me and said that Archbishop Michael
Francis sent them to find me in light of my earlier
application. They said they were not sure if I would
want to work with their health clinic, which was
also in rural Liberia. I immediately accepted the
offer. They shared some concerns regarding nurses
not wanting to work in rural Liberia. I assured
them that nothing would make me change my
mind. Even though my first choice was St. Joseph's
Catholic Hospital in Monrovia, my desire to give
back to the Catholic Church in Liberia by offering
my services as a nurse remained unchanged. The
Church had offered me immense financial support, from senior high school through the training for my professional nursing career. Therefore,
no geographical location would matter, as long as
the area was habitable. The nuns seemingly felt
relieved.

Shortly, I started work as a graduate nurse (GN)
under the direct supervision of the Director of
Nursing while I waited for my state board results.
After passing my state boards, I became a staff

nurse/clinician, then a charge nurse, and also the mobile clinic coordinator. In the latter capacity, we took clinical services to those who did not have the means of traveling for treatment. Areas commonly visited were the nearby and far away villages that had no access to commercial transport due to very bad roads. During mobile clinic visits, we provided preventive and curative services.

Towards the end of my first year of work at the Catholic health clinic, the nuns returned to my nursing alma mater for two more nurses. I felt much more reassured and empowered—W. J. Harley was indeed a school to attend! I worked at the clinic for five years.

CHAPTER TWO

College Years and the Liberian Civil War

I MOVED TO BONG COUNTY, ANOTHER area of rural Liberia. There, I went to join my husband at Cuttington: Cuttington University College. He had just returned from the United States of America with his graduate degree in Mental Health. I would soon begin my undergrad studies in Nursing. Yes, I would be doing my BSN— bachelor's degree in Nursing. Prior to starting school at the Cuttington University College, I got employed at the Phebe Medical Hospital as a staff nurse on the Medical/Surgical ward. I occasionally floated on the Pediatric ward, as needed. During my first performance evaluation, I got recommendations both from pediatrician Dr. Yvonne Takyi and a few other doctors on the Medical/Surgical ward. They wanted me transferred to the emergency room as the supervisor.

Soon, I found myself in multiple capacities—a student, a wife, a mother, and an employee; nonetheless, things seemed to be going well. And then, sometime later, an unusual event landed in the country—the start of a civil war that would shake the very foundation of the nation. That was during my second year at Cuttington. The war-related news began trickling in, building up around Bong County from the Ivory Coast, a neighboring West African country. By 1990, the war was in full tide. That way, our household began to plan an escape.

Prior to meeting my husband, he'd produced four children—Wilson, Yassah, Kokulo, and Marzey. In April 1990, they decided that they would go with Nyanquoi, their maternal uncle who lived in Lofa County, another leeward county of the country. I conferred with their father, and he said: "Lena, I do not want to stop them. But they should bear in mind that if things get worse, I may have no way of reaching them." Shortly, their bags were packed. We bade each of them goodbye and they left. Sometime later, we would reunite in strange circumstances. For the moment, however, we, the rest of the Franklin household, continued to live at Cuttington, Gbarnga.

By May 1990, however, I and the rest of the household fled to Monrovia. The thinking was that the capital city would be a haven. The day we arrived in Monrovia was the very day my mother, with whom we had thought to take refuge, left for Totota, another town in Bong County. Who cannot now marvel about the presence of cellphones! Had it been a part of life at that time, the appropriate planning would have been done. In any case, being a trader in used clothing, Mom left on a commercial trip. She reassured us that she would be out there for about one week. The home increased to sixteen individuals: my siblings, their children, a maternal uncle, the one who had not been well, one brother-in-law, my children, and me.

In the absence of my mother, I soon became the lone breadwinner. I dare say that sometimes the burden which one individual of means bears in developing countries is not enviable at all. Because someone had to keep our home at Cuttington to fend off possible looters in the wartime days, my husband returned to Cuttington after dropping us off at my mother's home in a neighborhood known as Bong Mines Bridge. The larger community was Bushrod Island. Liberia being settled by African Americans who had long left America after the end of slavery, Bushrod Island was one of their historical footprints.

Meantime, war-related tension continued to build up in the capital city. Fear of the unknown became palpable. One day, I decided to travel back home to Bong County to see how my husband was doing. Luckily, commercial transport was still available between Monrovia and several parts of rural Liberia. By midday, I got to the parking station. It was at Waterside, one of the sprawling marketplaces in Monrovia. There was just one overloaded van, I was told. The transport union, a body which often coordinated drivers' interactions with passengers, had decided to close at noonday every day. That way, drivers would avoid late hours of travel and therefore avoid any tragic eventualities possible during the crawling war.

While I was at the parking station, I saw a taxi. It was loaded with some goods. Besides the goods, there was a lone female passenger who, I realized, had chartered the taxi. She turned down my request to share her seat and therefore the cost. Obviously, I felt so bad for arriving at the parking station very late. Thereafter, I decided to return to Bong Mines Bridge and then plan to return to Waterside early the next morning. So, the next day, early in the morning, I left our refuge for the parking station before the last vehicle left for the day. Upon my arrival, I learned that the vehicles that left the day before were caught in an ambush in Kakata, about an hour's drive from Monrovia. Advancing rebels invaded the area, leading to the closure of all major roads from civilian travel. And then, it dawned on me—Had I left and got caught as had happened in the case of the previous vehicles, how would the huge number of people—sixteen mouths to feed!—in our transient home have weathered the storm, especially with my baby who was one and a half years old? All I could say at the moment was: "Every disappointment is surely a blessing!"

The days came, the days went. Uncertainties increased. One day, I went to central Monrovia to fetch for food and sundry items. Trying to return home to Bushrod Island, I realized there was no commercial vehicle. Almost everyone was on foot hurrying home. The breaking news was that the Independent Patriotic Front of Liberia (INPFL) had entered the nation's capital city! INPFL was one of just two major factions in the early part of the war. It had become a faction that peeled off the heretofore lone rebel group, which was the National Patriotic Front of Liberia (NPFL) being led by Charles Taylor. Conversely, the INPFL was being led by Prince Johnson. This INPFL had entered Monrovia via Bushrod island.

Bushrod Island is detached from mainland Monrovia by the Mesurado River. Two bridges connect the island to the mainland. In about two miles from any of those bridges, a traveler arrives at the nation's busiest port area. The port is known as the Freeport of Monrovia. When I got to the port, there was virtually no vehicle except for one pickup truck from the opposite direction, driving with neck-breaking speed. Aboard the truck, we traveling pedestrians learned, were wounded soldiers headed to central Monrovia; they were identified as AFL soldiers—that is, members of the Armed Forces of Liberia, yes soldiers of the national government.

I continued walking the nearly four-mile distance home from the Freeport of Monrovia. As I got closer to the Jamaica Road neighborhood, it became prudent to avoid the main route which was now being plied by the few recklessly speeding vehicles ferrying wounded soldiers and other army personnel. I found myself taking routes I used to take years earlier when I had newly arrived in Monrovia to pursue my middle school and senior high school education. It is really interesting how each year, as long as we live, there are moments that bring us back, mentally or physically, to where our lives began. As it is often said, "Wonders will never end!"

Many of us walking towards Bong Mines Bridge, Point Four, New Kru Town, Caldwell, or Duala, trekked through Seyon Town, and then Logan Town. It was as if there were instructions from some celestial force. In life, it seems that the fear of death has a way of instructing us all on evasive channels and strategies. Life with all its disquieting moments still remains a space to be occupied and paradoxically relished. The trekking seemed spontaneous. In the Bong Mines Bridge neighborhood, there is a police station. As I got close to the station, after which my mother's home would come in sight, I seemed the only one walking on that narrow path. In a minute, a few AFL soldiers appeared. They stood distance apart from one another. One of them asked me where I was headed. When I told him, he decided to escort me. A few yards past the back of the police station, I realized the entire neighborhood was even quieter. Every door remained closed; every home, dead silent. Racked by fright, I simply thanked the soldier as I trotted to a door.

No, it was not my home door. Are you kidding me? Tactical diversion was at work! I knocked so hard on the door calling one of my neighbors—a couple, Mr. & Mrs. Francis Kpankpai. I identified myself. They immediately opened the door. I entered and saw everyone lying on the floor, taking cover. In whispers, they told me that the rebels had penetrated the neighborhood. The couple told me that there had been intense rounds of shooting, which had just subsided. I was worried about my children and siblings. Mom's home was not very far from the Kpankpais', but the environment did not seem safe for me to continue home. After a while we heard movements, people talking; then someone in the house peeked through a window and said, "People are moving with their personal belongings."

I lost it! I did not know what to think, hoping and praying that my siblings did not leave home with my kids. If they did, where would I possibly find them? People leaving their homes, not knowing where some of them were headed! Thankfully, when I got home, everyone was there. I also met one of my few life-long friends who had stopped by to visit before the shooting started. I believed that this special presence gave my siblings a great deal of reassurance. It made them stick around while a dozen others fled from their homes for unknown destinations for "safety". Since then, I have thought about it. What I got from that moment was that sometimes God has a way of dispatching "angels" that bring us calm, resolve, and perhaps relief. Any wonder then, that it's often said that we are all the limbs of God Almighty?

"KNOWLEDGE IS POWER." IT'S been often said. Under the prevailing civil war circumstance, my knowledge and skills in nursing helped me skill-fully handle my family's health incidences as they unfolded. This was a time that I most cherished my nursing profession. Before enrolling into nursing school, I was told that nurses are underpaid, and that nursing is a very "poorly paid profession." Today, I beg to differ. I believe that nursing is surely a very rich profession. Nothing surpasses the relief one brings to the faces of those who otherwise go around with hanging faces because of needless, unabating pain. The smiles that light up are simply priceless.

Prior to our flight to Monrovia, I was fortunate to have packaged enough first aid medications and sundry supplies. Being a well experienced Registered Nurse at the time, my family survived from minor medical conditions through preven-tive and curative measures. No doubt, God, my God, does take the greatest portion of the glory, considering the path through which he has con-tinued to navigate my life.

At a time when hospitals, clinics, and major phar-macies/drug stores were shut down during the rising tension of the civil crises, managing health conditions at home was an immense challenge. The health conditions were vast and varied—Convulsions related to fever; signs and symptoms of malaria (at times with episodes of severe nausea and vomiting); severe toothaches associated with tooth decay/dental cavities; skin issues including open wounds. Syncope and diarrhea were also on the list. Even one of my sisters was, at the time, pregnant in her first trimester; she had to be attended to. I also had to make sure preventative measures were observed by all in the household.

As fighting intensified among NPFL, INPFL, and the AFL, I made several attempts to leave Monrovia with my children and other members of the family. My first thought was to go through the company site—i.e., through the Bong Mines company site. This would mean walking along the available train tracks. While all these thoughts were boiling in my mind, I continued to fetch for food to feed the family. One day, while on my way to search for food at a market, I heard one of the INPFL rebels call me by name. I and a few other pedestrians were passing one of the checkpoints found virtually everywhere in those days. This checkpoint was planted at a junction, the Caldwell-Bong Mines Bridge junction.

Now, it needs to be remembered that during the war, most of the rebels practiced the culture of disguise. They wore wigs, they wore masks, they sometimes painted their faces—just doing whatever it took to remain mysterious and frightening. Understandably, I couldn't recognize the face of this rebel. I answered and asked for his name.

He said, "I'm from Gbarnga—St. Martin's High School. Me and your children used to attend St. Martin. Don't worry-o. Y'aw wey soon go back to Gbarnga, riding cars. This operation will soon be over."

It was as if the guy knew what I was thinking before coming on the road to find food. Then I opened up to him with my plan of wanting to travel on foot along the railroad.

"Don't try it, Old Ma," he said. "NPFL soldiers are everywhere in the bush' along the train track, raping and killing innocent people. Don't worry, y'aw wey soon ride car to go back."

A week later, at about midnight, the sound of a huge bomb blast yanked us off beds. We fled outdoors. There was much chattering. At last, we saw a huge blaze of fire. It was from a house of twelve occupants, torched by the bomb just opposite us across the train track. This, at that hour of the night, got people fleeing their homes towards Bomi or beyond. In my temporary refuge, our things were always packed. At dawn, after the bombing incident, we took off for Kakata. The idea was that we would eventually make it to Gbarnga. This was a feat—not less than a week's walk on foot!

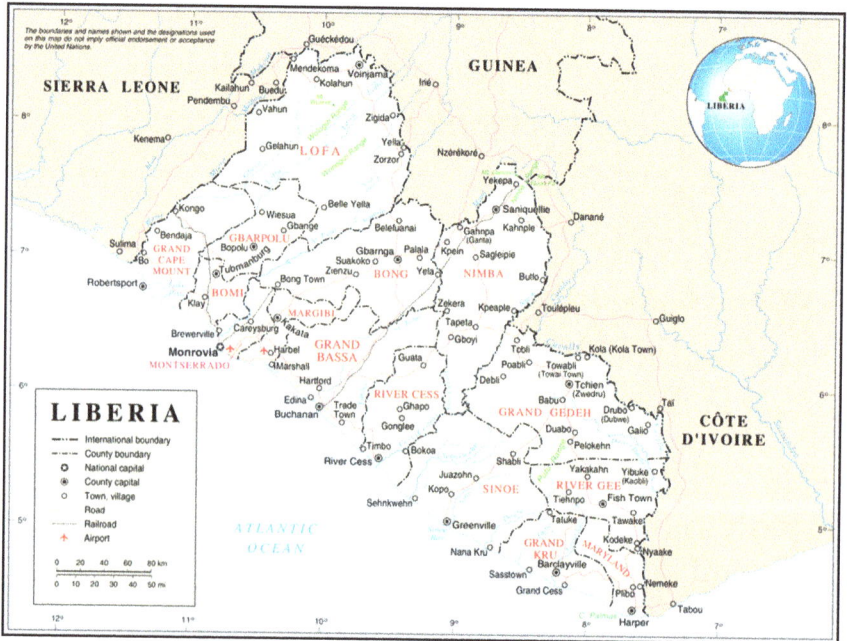

A map of Liberia featuring some of the places we walked through, fleeing from Monrovia, the nation's capital.

We took off. From Bong Mines Bridge to Duala, which is about a mile, we met many other people leaving Monrovia, heading west. For a while, my brother, Wilfred Sunday, we simply know as Sunday, decided he would escort us up to a distance and then return home—Mom's home. He held the large cooler which contained some of the food items that we were carrying. He also held some of the utensils we had on hand.

I held David Franklin, Jr., alias Noggie, on my back. At that time, he was just one and a half years old. As if that were not enough, Delcina Franklin, alias Sweetie, his elder sister, three years old, was by my side, her hand firmly in that of her five-year-old brother, Joe Kota Franklin's. The rest of my traveling group included my siblings, each with a little bundle. We were headed for Gbarnga, Bong County, trekking through Virginia and then Bensonville named Bentol during the years of President William Tolbert who had been deposed through a military coup in April 1980. Tolbert had been killed in the incident.

Wilfred continued to show much generosity. Often, he would walk ahead, start some rapport with those he met resting, leave his load with some of them and walk back to us to take Sweetie on his shoulder until we all got to the traveling group keeping watch over his load. We kept going like that until Wilfred reached a point of no return. Once we got in the area where Charles Taylor's NPFL reigned supreme, Wilfred could not turn around and head back for Bong Mines Bridge. The Taylor fighters would accuse him of being on reconnaissance or harboring different intentions (DI), a charge that could result in death on any unlucky day.

Later, we arrived in Virginia, a name reflective of the African American footprints in Liberia. In this area, we saw a Baptist church building. By this building stood a man who walked towards us and greeted us. He seemed to be a resident in the area. He appeared calm and concerned.

"Where are you coming from? Where are you going?" he asked.

"From Monrovia, trying to find our way to Gbarnga," I answered.

"Are you traveling with any sharp utensil(s) or instruments?" He still spoke in a calm voice.

Whether out of naivete or simply by a gut response, I said we had what he'd asked for. He advised that we left them in the area because if rebels ahead found them upon checking our loads, it would mean death or some terrible punishment. In short, traveling with silent weapons was as much a danger as carrying brazen weapons. Wilfred was with us and not ahead of us. We got out the forks and kitchen knives and gave them to the unknown man. I also told him thanks for being very kind with such important, life-saving information.

By late afternoon we made it to Bensonville and were accommodated in a very big house attached to a huge palaver hut/town hall where we met many other displaced Liberians. We learned that that was Charles Taylor's compound. We made ourselves comfortable after eating some farina, a local cereal often eaten by stirring in sugar or palm oil. We passed the night.

At the break of day, we resumed our journey with others traveling the same route. We walked for about another whole day. As we got closer to another town before reaching Careysburg, it was curfew time; therefore, we couldn't go any further

but to spend the night. Careysburg, another historical footprint of African Americans in Liberia, was
founded in 1856 and named for Rev. Lott Carey,
the first American Baptist missionary to Africa
and a key figure in the founding of Liberia. It is
located about 15 miles northeast of Monrovia.

I should say here, though, that the African
American sector of the Liberian population long
settled the land and became known by historians
as "pioneers," "settlers," or "Americo Liberians,"
whereas the Africans they met on the land became
known later as "indigenous Liberians." For 133
years, these settlers ruled the country in ways that
eventually led to a military coup in April 1980. I
happened to be of the indigenous Liberian sector.

Prior to reaching Careysburg, we passed through
a checkpoint at a Voice of America (VOA) instal-
lation. At that checkpoint, we were all ordered
to walk single-filed, during which each of us was
questioned. Some of us were accused of being on
surveillance or reconnaissance from the Armed
Forces of Liberia. In a moment of time, one of
the rebels walked up to the line. My heart missed
a beat. Well, it turned out that he did not seem

to mean any harm. He said he was once a police officer from Tappita where I had worked with the Catholic Health Clinic. Many in the area referred to me as "Doctor Woman."

Here, I felt a little relaxed and reassured. The man dashed off. When he returned, he brought a gallon of icy cold water with a glass for my children and me. Then, he led me and my traveling group to one of the fighters' temporary tents nearby to take a seat. He introduced me to his commander, stating that I was a "doctor" in Tappita. Now, I've always known better than ride high with some honorific title. I have been confident about my range of knowledge and skills in the health profession, especially in the nursing profession. However, I do know my place in this health industry. Those professionals who will not know their place in the sphere of a profession simply need to be very reflective.

How does a nurse differ from a doctor? From my own experience and the relevant available health literature, I'll tell you how. The differences begin with the question of training time. All relevant health literature shows that nurses train for years fewer than those of a doctor. For the baseline, nurses go for up to eight years of training, whereas doctors train up to eleven years, leading to specialization. Both nurses and doctors have to be licensed. Nurses work in a supportive role to doctors. Nurses are mainly patient-focused, whereas doctors are mainly disease-focused. This means that nurses focus on how to prevent diseases and therefore offer the relevant, continuous health education; doctors assess and treat diseases. Of course, both nurses and doctors can provide prognosis, they can order and interpret lab results, they can perform tests and prescribe the appropriate treatment. Nevertheless, nurses do not operate independent of doctors. In other words, nurses work under the supervision of doctors. Perhaps, I should add that under an ideal condition nurses and doctors working together can produce significant and protracted health results.

So, I was introduced to the commander on our long journey to Gbarnga. He was happy to meet me. He wanted to look through my personal belongings for medications he wanted. He already had a list at his fingertips. Most of what he wanted I had, and he attempted to take almost everything for himself—the shallowness of it all! I pleaded with him to leave some of the medications for my kids and me because we didn't know how long either our journey or the war would last.

Meantime, just a short distance from where we stood interacting, another rebel was manhandling Wilfred, my brother—unbeknownst to me! This rebel and some of his men grabbed that tall young man, a little over six feet, and tied him up at the elbows. In wartime, most Liberians knew that as "tabay." There, your arms were pulled back, with elbow touching elbow, and mercilessly tied with twine as if at any moment a butcher knife would be used to cut through your bare chest, up and down your sternum. Whenever some victims were relieved from that condition and depending on how long they'd been tied up, they never use their arms effectively again.

While on line, we were instructed that none should look back or answer for any fellow traveler—"Soldiers talk for themselves!" Such a silly logic! We were no soldiers, no fighters. We were simply ordinary people caught in the circumstances of life. I hadn't realized what was happening to my dear brother until it all became so glaring. They had pushed him out of the line and ordered him to step on to an elevated spot for execution. His height and build had rendered him suspect. No sooner had I seen what was unfolding than I screamed.

"That's my very own brother there, Commander!"

"Yeah? As you were, soldiers!" he said.

"Yes, Sir!"

At last, Wilfred was escorted to our tent and untied. Wilfred let out a traumatic sigh and stirred into space. He really looked terribly shaken. In the morning, we took off for Careysburg. We arrived at a rebel checkpoint at the intercession of Bentol and Careysburg. There, I was detained by the rebels. "Tito," their commander at the gate, gave orders to have me taken to their house just across the road. He wanted me for a wife! The fact that I stood there with my 18-month-old baby on my back, my other babies, 3- and 5-year-olds at my side, did not stir human dignity and decency in him. Now, as I describe the situation I found myself in, I simply need to chuckle: Just what was I thinking? How could I not understand the beast

most people become in the heat of such a phenomenon as war, especially war that really seeks to feed
the ugly cravings of humanity? Anyway, I pleaded
with him to let me go to join my brother and the
other members in my traveling group ahead. Tito
maintained that his bodyguard would take me to
the designated house.

He kept to his word. At the house, I met three
civilians (a husband, a wife, and a sister-in-law).
They had traveled from Fendell in search of their
young nephew missing while they were on their
way to Bong Mines. It seemed they knew some
of the rebels who were living in that house. They
told me about the kind of person Tito was—some
no-nonsense character he seemed to demonstrate.
I gave myself to God at that moment, reciting the
23rd Psalm, alternating that with a quiet recitation
of the Holy Rosary. Meantime, I managed to send
Francis, my little boy of the April 1975 days, to
walk along the straight route in search of Wilfred.
They met while Wilfred was on his way back to get
Sweetie. He got the news that we couldn't continue
the journey. Wilfred went back to the rest stop,
collected the cooler, and joined us.

Gbolu and the couple that we met in the house offered us some cooked food—specifically, cassava leaf and rice, of the many Liberian delicacies. I had lost my appetite. The children ate. I took a walk on the back porch, sitting there praying the Rosary quietly. While I was in the torturous mood, I saw one of the rebels enter the back porch. I really didn't know where he was coming from. He wore some regalia, a cross over between an academic and a choir gown. He complemented that with a wig on his head—one of the weird forms of rebel dress code: dress in a strange way and look mysterious or look frightening. He greeted me and then started to question me. Where was I coming from? Where was I going? Length of stay in Monrovia? What was my mission there? Why did I leave (from Monrovia)? He seemed unknown to stopping the series of what I thought frivolous questions. Well, what did I know! Perhaps, he wanted to satisfy his security-related curiosity. Shortly after the questions that seemed endless, he told me to follow him inside of the house so he would see my children. As we entered, he called me by a familiar name "Doctor Woman," as I was commonly called during my Tappita years. I had worked out there for five consecutive years. God is faithful! Obviously, the name caught my attention. Somewhat relieved, I asked for the man's name.

"I am Jack Mint," a name, I'd prefer here. "My brother was Frank Mint," another preferred name. "Frank was friendly with Sarah at the clinic. I attended St. Gabriel High. One time I got hurt during a volleyball game and you treated me. My parents always spoke highly of you each time they visited the clinic. You were very nice. As for that Tito man who sent you here as his woman, I will never allow him to mess with you as he does with other women. I'm his commander. So, do not worry. You and your children will sleep at my place."

Jack was still talking to me when Tito entered.

"Where is my woman?! Where is my woman?!"

Suddenly, he recognized Jack's presence. Without another word he stood at attention and saluted Jack. It was heartwarming to see the display of hierarchy! *So, Jack was really the head of this Tito fool!* I heard Jack warn him: "This woman is a doctor who helped our people in Tappita. She is not

one of those you'll bring in here and thrash afterwards. Make sure you secure a ride for her and her
children tomorrow. She is CIC (Commander-in-
Chief's) guest." The labeling reference to Charles
Taylor, the overall commander of NPFL, often
restrained every single rebel.

"Yes, Sir!" Tito said.

My suppressed joy at the moment was bound-
less. Shortly after the conversation, Jack told me
that he would come later in the evening to pick up
my children and me to spend the night at his place.
And then in the morning, he would prepare a pass/
clearance for us and put us on a dump truck, one
of few vehicles at the time, to leave for Kakata and
then transition to Gbarnga, our destination.

You will therefore understand how terrible I felt
when a heavy rain started pouring an hour after
Jack left. The rain lasted for hours. How the human
mind fashions a legion of ugly images to drown a
fearful soul! Fright ate through me—to think I'd
spend a night in the same house with Tito! To my
relief, Jack returned at about 11pm when all the
children had fallen asleep. He did not come with
a vehicle; therefore, he advised that we remained

where we were for the night and that he would prepare a pass for us in the morning. God was at work and I continued to put my trust in Him. He seemed to keep in my corner.

Late in the night while we were asleep, sharp beams of moonlight shot through the glass windows almost like fluorescent light. It was a perfect light in place of electricity. After midnight, my youngest baby and I got into a bed that was offered to me, while the other kids and my siblings slept on some blankets on the floor. Sometime later, I noticed a male figure entering the room. He got in the bed, with my baby in the center. My heart began to pound like it would bolt out of my chest. I was very frightened but lay still. I began to pray silently against any possible abuse. I kept watching for what this sleazy man's next move would be. He tapped me on my chest and told me to move my baby to my opposite side. That way, I would be ever close to possibly preparing myself to feed his base appetite. I could not recognize the face but for sure that was not Tito. Hearing his request, I summoned courage and sat up. I looked at him. Then, I asked in a very calm but firm tone:

"What if I were your mother or your sister, defenseless, and you my son or brother—imagine hearing that a man wants to do or has done what you are planning to do right now. How would you feel? I want you to be very honest in answering the question. And just think before you answer." I saw him drag himself to a sitting position. He sat at the edge of the bed, avoiding my face.

"I am sorry," he said almost in whispers, and then I watched him stand up and put his hand over a shoe rack close by the bed. He handed me a blanket and a flashlight saying, "It gets cold during the early morning hours. Use the blanket to cover you and your baby. Have this flashlight, in case you or the children want to use the bathroom outside. The inside toilet is completely out of order."

"The moonlight will go away."

"Thanks," I said. In seconds, he quietly walked out of the room.

I think about the interaction today and do believe that there really is something called conscience. It is perhaps the God in all of us, no matter the situation or condition in life. The challenge in our human world is how to find the knob to flip on that feeling, which is another name for the conscience, that whispers: "Yes, you know—this person could be me. This person could be someone I could die for. This person is me. I'd better splash and swim in the very feeling this person is carrying right now. I really must!" Could it be what Christ had in mind when he urged: "Do unto others as you would like them do unto you?" It's something to really think about in a world that seems to be rocking and breaking apart over needless anger and hatred.

At about 7am, Jack came over with a pass, stamped and signed by him as clearance for my siblings, my kids, and me to go to Kakata. The roads leading from Fendell through Bentol were very busy with the mass exodus of people heading to different destinations: Careysburg, Kakata, Bong Mines, Gbarnga, Nimba, etc. Firestone dump trucks, snatched from the Harvey S. Firestone Rubber Plantation, were headed towards Fendell, evidently transporting civilians. Jack told Tito to make sure to tell the drivers to leave a space for eight people ready to be picked up on the way back. He obeyed. Around noon the trucks were returning and were filled to capacity with people. Jack waited and made sure we got on one of the trucks to Kakata. While we awaited the truck, Jack asked if I could stay with them to be their Nurse, and that he would ask "CIC," really referring to Charles Taylor, to open a clinic in Careysburg for me to run or coordinate.

"That would be nice," I said. "You guys are doing very well and need necessary medical care. But let me take my children home to their father on Cuttington, and I will return in a few days."

He decided to send me with an escort to bring me back to them safely.

"Don't worry," I said. "God will make my return possible and safe."

"Can you leave your wedding band with me to make sure you will come back?"

"This ring is very tight on my finger," I told him. "I sure will return."

"Don't worry. I believe you. I trust you."

We took off for Kakata. But before we took off, Tito and his boys packed foodstuff—a quarter bag of rice, farina, palm oil, salt, etc.—for us to take along. And then, we left. After sometime, we arrived near Kakata. Everyone on the truck was dropped off on the campus of one of the few vocational/technical, middle level training institutions in the country. It was an institution named for Booker T. Washington of the United States of America. BWI campus is somewhat on the outskirts of Kakata. In the war years, this campus was a spot for screening. Often, people were screened upon arriving and leaving Kakata. When we arrived on the campus, Wilfred became ill with high fever. I got to work immediately. I commenced treatment for malaria. Later, his fever broke, and he rested very well.

My children, siblings, and I were favored and never went through any screening lines when we got on BWI campus. At some point, I heard some-one call the familiar name, "Doctor Woman."

"Doctor Woman, where are you coming from and where are you going? How many persons are you traveling with? Follow me let me give you some foodstuff and show you where you and your family will sleep."

Again, this was another NPFL fighter from Tappita who explained my importance to his col-leagues about my work of helping his people in

Tappita when I worked at the clinic prior to the war. In the shortest possible time, he supplied us with a quarter bag of rice, palm oil, salt, pepper, and Bouillon cubes. Then he showed us a dormitory to spend the night or simply use for the rest of the time we intended to stay in the area. For the first time since our journey from Monrovia, we cooked, took bath, ate to our satisfaction, and slept very soundly. The farther we were away from Monrovia, the more peaceful the atmosphere seemed.

The next day, we woke up after a very restful night. Our journey continued from BWI to Kakata itself for a possible ride to Gbarnga. At the BWI exit, there was another checkpoint for NPFL. Here, everyone was screened before leaving the campus. Again, my family and I were spared. We weren't screened because of the former Tappita resident, the NPFL soldier who was one of the area commanders that took us through their gates to town.

Upon arriving in central town, Kakata, we met hundreds of people, some of whom were people we knew. There were homes made available for those of us displaced and for those who were searching for transport vehicles to get to various destinations.

Obtaining a pass/clearance was a requirement
to board any vehicle leaving Kakata. I was told
that medical director, Dr. Walter Gwenigale, was
sending a truck each day to pick up residents or
employees of Phebe Hospital. I was also told that
the Red Cross had an office in Kakata providing
food for the displaced people as well as contact-
ing family members via radio communication. I
met a familiar staff, Bill Caranda. He gave us some
ration, contacted my husband, and told him that
the kids and I were in Kakata.

From the Red Cross office, I went to the NPFL's
transport union office to obtain a pass for Gbarnga
as was required before boarding any vehicle from
Kakata. There was a very long queue. However,
operating with some degree of urgency, I decided
to bypass and enter the office, with my baby on
my back. The sun was spewing out its tropical
heat.

I saw one of the guards approaching me with
a gun, asking me what I wanted. I was very calm
and explained why I bypassed the line. He told
me to see him by 12:30pm at a house across the
road from their office. He promised to expedite

the process. I agreed. With fear and hope, I went to see him later . I got there at 12:45pm and met a group of fighters sitting in a circle smoking marijuana. The man was not in the group. My fear level started to rise, not knowing what to expect. As I was about to leave, they asked who I was looking for. Unfortunately, I didn't know the guy's name. Just then, I saw him enter and explain that I was out there to see him. He immediately prepared the pass with their stamp and told me to find "something for him." All I had in my purse was thirty-five Liberian dollars. He accepted the money and told me that he helped me because I looked like his missing mother. They'd separated. That was how he joined the fighting group, hoping he would find her somewhere one day. I said I was sorry about that.

"Please pray for me to find her one day."

"I sure will," I said and then left.

BY NOW, SOME OF our Cuttington University College neighbors that we met in Kakata had made arrangements with one of the commanders who was running a clandestine transport scheme during very late hours, between 2am and 5am. The scheme was to meet him at his house at 12am. We got to his house and he wasn't there. We waited until late dawn. He didn't show up. Later in the day, we arranged with a Volkswagen bus by which we took off from Kakata. Just as we entered Totota, one of the tires punctured—where? In the neighborhood of where my mother, we learned, was residing! I took the time to check around for her while the tire was being repaired. OMG, I found her! She couldn't believe her eyes, seeing us from Monrovia and considering the prevailing war situation in the country. See how long her one week stay out of Monrovia had turned into! She was overwhelmed with joy, just as we were.

ONE AND A HALF hours of repair time later, we bade her farewell and got back on the road. The driver dropped us at the Phebe Hospital compound. He said that he was not going further. From Phebe to our house on Cuttington was 30 minutes away. Considering the times, and considering the length we had traveled, the distance left was much shorter.

Life at CUC was still at some comfortable peak. There was electricity still around the clock. We got home around the evening. We were swept into joy, tears running down faces. At Cuttington, it was really clear that Taylor's NPFL had a strong-hold. The fighting forces spread all over, making Cuttington a part of their base. Surprisingly, I found a part of my extended family at Cuttington. There had been an orphanage known as the Fatima Cottage. The owner of the Cottage was an in-law of my paternal grandmother. She had been living at the Cottage shortly before the war. Charles Taylor who had found favor with the proprietress had uprooted the entire Cottage occupants to his base in Gbarnga. Among the occupants were a young cousin and his two friends. All three did not want to stay on Taylor's dorms. Life was throbbing again.

CHAPTER THREE

New Life Begins…Not So Fast!

MY FAMILY STARTED A NEW LIFE. But I have to say that things were tightening up. War-induced poverty was setting in. I thought to begin petty trading. I made children clothes for sale; caustic soda soap for sale; and then fritters, which we locally call *kala*. Instead of flour, I used grated cassava. The kala also went for sale. I kept doing all that until we returned to Phebe Hospital to begin formal work. When we began, salaries were not paid in full. In lieu of full salaries, food supplies were provided to employees periodically.

My husband and his friends often collected old tires and tire tubes to make simple sandals and slippers that were once fashionable in the days of nationwide campaigns for social change in the 1970s. These footwears were named for Liberian economist Togba Nah Tipoteh who popularized them in those years to infuse in ordinary people the need to learn to live within their means. In the war years which began in the late 1980s, the Tipoteh footwears became another source of income. My husband and his friends would load up their wheelbarrows and travel to the nearby villages to trade some of the Tipoteh for fish, meat, oil, and some farm produce. Barter system was in full swing!

Yet, when life seems adjustable, especially during war years, everything then quickly falls apart. As the war intensified, the world could not ignore the massive diseases and deaths occurring in Liberia, West Africa. Through regional bodies in Africa, it now became time for the Economic Community of West African States to come in. A peace command comprising of peacekeeping contingents from ECOWAS, known as Ecomog, was established. Ecomog was empowered to monitor peace in the country. Any faction failing to comply had to face the full weight of Ecomog. With a fleet of jet fighters, Ecomog got to work. The planes were swift and a no-nonsense type. The rebels feared them tremendously. Most Liberians in the country called them "Dodo Birds." In minutes, they would speed from nearby Sierra Leone, deposit their hot eggs in trouble zones and then fly back to base. Many Liberians, too, fearing that they could become part of the collateral damage, decided it was time to leave the country.

In a few days filled with anxiety, we'd flee from our homes in the early morning hours, as a matter of popular tactic, to spread through nearby expanse of rubber trees and then return in the evening. The whole thing was often confusing and disturbing, for we never knew exactly when any of these bombers would fly in. The word was that the jet bombers often sought to identify crowds and residential areas. For some reason, it was said that such scenes were suggestive of trouble spots. Whether that explanation was propaganda or not, wherever the saving of dear life was involved, we were usually determined simply to take cover in the best way we knew how, whenever we heard Dodo Bird in the air.

In those tension-ridden days, an incident shook our spines. That day, employees were returning from work. I got on the hospital bus to go to the central market/shopping center in Gbarnga while day shift workers were being dropped home. During this time, nurses from first shift work sessions often purchased their groceries and then returned with the bus to their homes when the bus had completed the drop off of employees. Just as I got off the bus with another nurse who went to Gbarnga for the same shopping purpose, we spotted the bombers—within minutes! Seconds later, bombs were dropped on the radio station from where the rebel leader Charles Taylor had been spewing his revolutionary propaganda. Only God knew whatever collateral damage was not caused in the process.

That day, a colleague and I took cover together. Later, we found ourselves at the nearby St. Martin's Catholic Mission. We were accommodated by the then Archbishop Dotu Seekey in the guesthouse opposite the parish house. He was the very cleric who many years earlier flew me from Harper to Sasstown after my health treatment at the J. J. Dossen Hospital. At the St. Martin's Catholic Mission, I remember him teasing: "Helena are you coming from the battle front?" I guess he saw how my white uniform looked soiled from taking cover. I had unabashedly rolled under old cars and nearby market tables as the bombers either flew by or circled about. We had dinner with the archbishop and other parish staff. My colleague and I spent a very comfortable night at the parish guesthouse. The next day, the Christian gentleman took us home, dropped me off at CUC and my colleague off at Phebe. Archbishop Sekey would die many years later.

The war intensified and the toll of casualties continued to rise. One day, a group of Catholic nuns arrived at the Phebe Hospital. I realized I had worked with them about two and a half years earlier when I worked in Tappita. As you will expect, it was a heartwarming reunion. However, the joy was short-lived. This day, they were not on a joyous trip; they were traveling in an ambulance and returning to Tappita from Monrovia. That was before what would be known in the Liberian civil war history as the Lutheran Church Massacre.

The nuns stopped by with a little girl who was about a year and a few months old. Somewhere in an area called Paynesville, a suburb of Monrovia, they'd spotted the baby securely tied onto the back of her mother who was facing down into the earth.

The baby was fighting for relief; after all, the mother had been shot fatally in the back—one of the mysteries of life. How was it possible that the little girl, too, was not shot dead? The nuns, realizing what was happening, went over and untied the child. They checked the mother and noted she was stone dead. They then took the child, realizing that she too had been wounded in the right leg. The thigh and hip had been fractured and dislocated. They fitted her with a splint to stabilize the affected leg.

Delivered to us for treatment, we went to work, continuing to provide her with much-needed care. We named her Baby Phebe. She fully recovered and lived on the pediatric ward for over two years because she had no relative to claim her. Later, though, the hospital found it prudent to find adoption for her. It was unsafe for her to spend her healthy life in the confines of this health center through which illnesses of all kinds flowed. We were glad that the little girl was eventually taken into a loving home. So ended the story of a dead woman with a live baby tied to her back.

More victims were to come. Many war victims were brought into the hospital via the ER—

emergency room. These were mainly rebels from the battlefield. At about this time, a family friend blamed the medical staff for prolonging the war.

"Why?" I asked.

"You people treat the fighters, safe their lives, and they return to the battlefield, killing innocent people, looting, and threatening them."

I reminded her that we took an oath before God and in the presence of an assembly and promised to remain loyal in our duties. I wish I'd have poured out lines of "The Florence Nightingale Pledge" with sparkling and reassuring words, such as *pledge, purity, faithfully, loyalty, maintain, elevate, the standard of my profession,* like sparks flying off and lighting the dark:

> I solemnly pledge myself before God and in the presence of this assembly, to pass my life in purity and to practice my profession faithfully. I will abstain from whatever is deleterious and mischievous, and will not take or knowingly administer any harmful drug. I will do all in my power to maintain and elevate the standard of my profession, and will

hold in confidence all personal matters committed to my keeping and all family affairs coming to my knowledge in the practice of my calling. With loyalty will I endeavor to aid the physician in his work, and devote myself to the welfare of those committed to my care.

Meantime, the victims kept coming. Some of the victims brought to the hospital came with self-inflicted wounds. It turned out that these were untrained fighters. Some died from ignorance, wounding themselves or their fellow rebels out of ignorance. At one point, one of them sustained a terrible bullet wound when he pressed his gun's trigger while looking through the muzzle of the gun. At another point, one of the fighters used his machine gun to literally kill a fly on the concrete floor, while he and his friends were eating. The bullets fired bounced off into his chest and other parts of his body, thus killing himself and badly wounding others who sat close to him.

And then, there was another fighter who mishandled a grenade. It exploded with particles inflicting serious wounds to parts of his genitalia.

That was the one who each time I went to treat his wounds believed he saw a woman for his groin! After some treatment, he was probably glad to disabuse himself of that mind.

Again, in such situations of the commonality of ailments, it seemed odd that enmity never lost its sting. Whereas health workers were busy caring for the sick and the wounded, even among the same sick and wounded, there were some evil-minded patients plotting to exact revenge on others, both for matters of ethnicity and for matters of religious affiliation.

It is appropriate, perhaps, to go back briefly to July 1990 when some troops of the Armed Forces of Liberia, at night, stormed the St. Peter's Lutheran Church in Sinkor, Monrovia, leading to the well-known Lutheran Church Massacre. The soldiers, allegedly of President Samuel Doe's ethnic group, entered the church compound to hunt out members of the ethnic groups who were kindred of an earlier deceased Thomas Quiwonkpa who had been Doe's archrival. By the time the incident ended, approximately 600 men, women, and children were killed on July 29, 1990. Not long, a few Catholic missionaries led by Fr. Larry Gilmore went on the scene, hoping that there might be some victims still alive. Fr. Gilmore had worked in rural Liberia. The mission was successful. They took several victims to the St. Joseph's Catholic Hospital. But realizing that the humanitarian gesture angered the Doe-led government, which was pursuing enemies, here and there, the Catholic Mission made a quick determination. The hospital had to be evacuated. Those patients that were within days of being discharged had to be discharged. Those who still had longer periods of stay at the hospital had to be taken elsewhere. Phebe Hospital, which is some five or six hours away from Monrovia, became the likely venue. It was behind NPFL lines.

At least fifty men, women, and children were transported by two buses through checkpoints upcountry to Phebe Hospital. Among them was a patient with one leg amputated, at the hip. He was not a fighter. He had been a cargo truck driver who had a near fatal accident prior to the war. Nevertheless, while he was at Phebe, there were a few fighters of a different ethnic group. Having identified his ethnic group, they began to plan how to snatch him away and kill him. The hospital learned of the plot and issued a warning.

Soon, the administrators found themselves helpless in the matter; they couldn't fend off these mali-
cious fighters. Failing to succeed, the administrators
got me and a few others together. At the head of the
team was Solomon ("Solo") Garpue, the adminis-
trative service person who often had his way with
the rebels, almost effortlessly pulling through
checkpoints. Some people really do have a way of
working their way through people and things, even
in risky times. Solo was one such individual. And
the hospital administration never failed to call on
him. We disguised the man and ferried him out of
the hospital and took him to the Guinea parking
station in Danane, the Ivory Coast, from where he
would go to his long-left home in Guinea. He did
really have a lingering regret over which he cried
bitterly. The regret and therefore deep fear was
that as a youth he had moved to Liberia and spent
most of his adult life there. He'd lost contact with
home and family. To whom and to where would
he be landing in such a frail condition as he was?
Well, Phebe Hospital had given him some spend-
ing money. Nothing more the hospital seemed prepared to do. It was really a sad moment for all of us.

A Flight from Liberia

BY 1991 OUR CUP of fright seemed filled to over-flowing. My children and I fled to Danane, the Ivory Coast. After we got there, I went to register my children at the PMRC (Protestant Methodist Resource Center) where Ms. Loretta Gruver was the school nurse and health educator. We met upon my arrival on the campus. We both were excited to see each other. After a brief conversation unrelated to job issues, she told me, "Helena, you've just got yourself a job. Now, I can return to America until the fighting in Liberia ceases." After a few days, she presented me the keys to the school clinic, following orientation with her. She also turned over to me the teaching materials for health education.

My family and I, then, began to settle in. One cold rainy morning, while at the United Nations High Commissioner for Refugees [UNHCR] center for ration, some friends and I were discussing what had been flowing out of BBC news. Young girls were being raped. Young boys were being recruited for various warring factions. And then, one of the friends said, "Oh, and they say it's worse in Lofa County. In fact, a girl by the name of Kebbeh just went and got her family from Guinea. They had crossed over from Lofa." Lofa County is one of several counties in Liberia.

As anyone following the story would guess, my antenna went up: the children! What was I to do then?—the father was still in Gbarnga. It became prudent to engage further with Ponawenie, the friend. I wanted her to connect me with Kebbeh. Maybe Kebbeh would give me an idea about how I could reach out to the children. Within a few days, Ponawenie was able to put me in touch with Kebbeh. We chatted and from all indications, Kebbeh knew the children and had an idea of their location in Lofa. She assured me that she could send a message to someone in Guinea to have them cross over into Guinea, following just about the same trail her family had followed.

Early the next morning, I went to a branch office of the Christian Health Association of Liberia (CHAL) in Danane, the Ivory Coast. CHAL was an organization he was working for at Phebe, the Suakoko branch office in Bong County, Liberia. The head office was in Monrovia, the nation's capital. We spoke on the radio; he immediately made arrangement with the Danane branch office to make funds available for me to start the process of getting the children from Lofa through Guinea as per the plan with Kebbeh. Within a week, Kebbeh was able to get the children over—along with Nyanquoi, the uncle. It was a heartwarming reunion.

Shortly, God guided us through an adjustment process as quickly as possible. I was able to enroll them at the Protestant Methodist Resource Center [PMRC]. At the time of their arrival, the first marking period had ended. Every marking period often ran for six weeks. Enrolling them wasn't too easy because it was late. But being on the faculty as the health educator and Nurse for the school clinic, things went well. I reassured the school administration of the children's ability to perform well. And then, they got to work, serious work. For the rest of the time during the war, we never separated again.

A year later, in 1992, we returned to Liberia. I returned to work at the Phebe Hospital in Suakoko. Shortly thereafter, my family and I moved to Monrovia, where I got employed with Don Bosco

Homes as General Health Services Coordinator and clinician with focus on war affected children—the abandoned, orphans, waywards, etc. Critically ill children were referred to the St. Joseph's Catholic Hospital. And yet, in 1994, my children and I returned to the Ivory Coast when another episode of the Liberian civil war erupted. Out there, I got rehired by the PMRC. The swing, one might say, continued. I returned to Liberia in 1996 when the fighting relatively ceased. I got rehired with DBH. In between the fighting episodes, CUC temporarily acquired a part of the John Fitzgerald Kennedy Hospital in Monrovia. This arrangement was intended to ensure that CUC seniors completed their studies in readiness for graduation. I was one of the seniors. In February of 1999, a convocation was held, and I graduated, Cum Laude!

Later that same year, I requested for a transfer from DBH (Don Bosco Homes) via the Catholic Secretariat to a sister institution MPCHS (Mother Pattern College of Health Sciences) as an instructor in the Nursing department for growth and development in my Nursing career. My transfer was granted and processed. Thus, in 2000, I joined

MPCHS, where I taught a number of courses—
Pediatric Nursing, Professional Ethics, Laboratory
Ethics, and Management in Nursing. I eventually
went to serve as Coordinator of a newly established Bachelor of Science program for nurses and
for physician assistants.

The map of Africa—My continent of origin

They were our pillars, so we became what we now are—
W. J. Harley, Ganta, Nimba County.

Attending a short farewell program in honor of Ms. Loretta Gruver. It was also the
day she officially turned over the keys to the school clinic, and the teaching mate-
rials for health education to me. Protestant Methodist Resource Center (PMRC),
Danane, Ivory Coast. Back row: L-R—Me and Ms. Gruver; Front row: L-R—Rev.
Brother Joseph and Rev. Brother Murray.

Celebrating Don Bosco Feast Day. Heading to the Don Bosco Youth Center, Matadi, Monrovia, Liberia, for an official program, games, and refreshments

A composite photo. Scene 1: L-R—Tappita, Nimba County: David K. Franklin, Sr., my husband; Mrs. Martha Reeves; and Me [1987]. We both had gone to visit Mrs. Reeves, a very loving woman. Scene 2: L-R—Monrovia [2001]: A student and me outside of the Don Bosco Polytechnic, after participating in a program climaxing a week-long set of activities for National Nurses. At the program, I presented the "Life of the Lady with the Lamp/the Mother of Nursing"—Florence!

Cuttington University College: How empowering and refreshing graduation feels! I'm at the far right.

Me and a close bud, Mrs. Sophie T. Parwon.

The Newly Minted BSN Cuttington University College

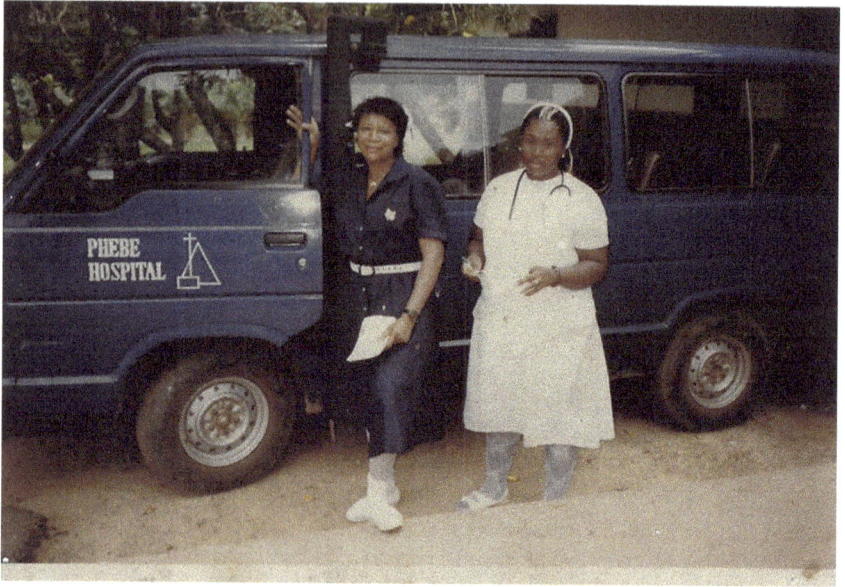

Me, a colleague (Mrs. Alice Hawa Salifu), and the ubiquitous Phebe Hospital van.

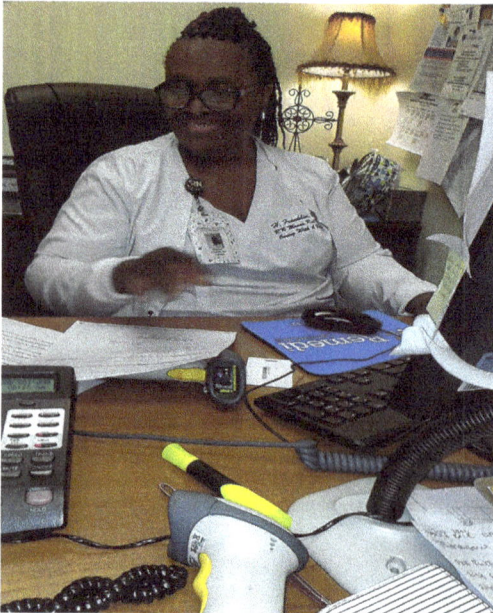

Taking charge!—At the Mother Angeline McCrory Manor-Skilled and Long-Term Care (MAMM).

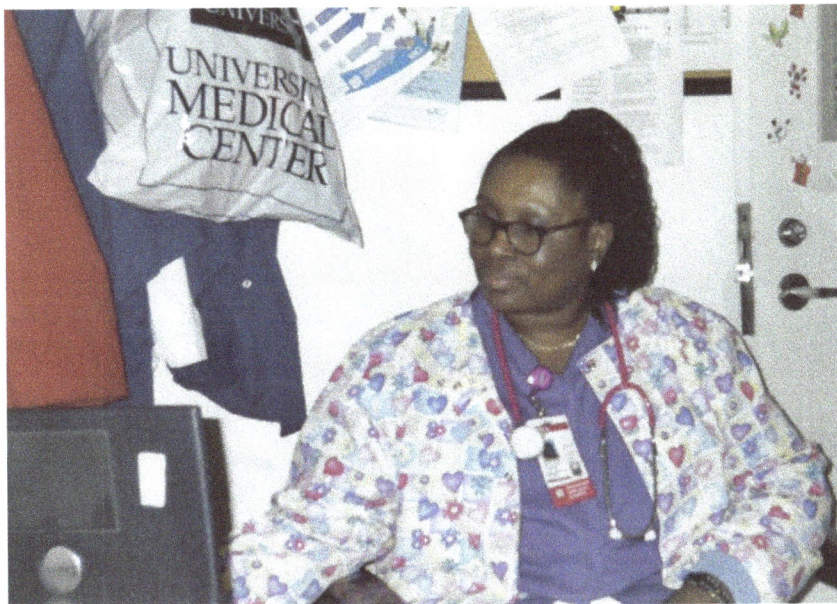

Documenting, using my computer—At the Ohio State University Medical Center, Columbus, OH.

At a shift change, receiving a report from the outgoing RN Supervisor—Lolita.

In the conference room, completing my report for a meeting in few minutes—MAMM, Columbus, Ohio.

In a faculty procession—Mother Pattern College of Health Sciences (MPCHS) Campus of Don Bosco Polytechnic, Monrovia, Liberia

Just give me a little break— A little funtime doesn't hurt, or does it!

So Life's Been!

CHAPTER FOUR

A Good Idea Can Stand on Its Own Legs

ONE DAY IN THE EARLY 1980s, at about 8pm, a young mother, let's call her Martha, arrived at a hospital where I served as a student nurse. She arrived with a problem for the emergency room. Her two-year-old son reportedly swallowed a nickel. The ER nurse assessed the little boy and found that he had no breathing problem. Additionally, all his vital signs were stable. So, the advice was that both mother and child went home, and that they kept monitoring the boy's bowel movement; perhaps, the boy would pass the nickel.

Upon getting the report and prior to the mother leaving with the child, Mabel, the Operating Room/ER Coordinator, a Registered Nurse, suggested x-rays of the boy's chest and abdominal. That way, we would determine the exact location of the nickel. The on-call MD was also called and updated. The decision for the x-rays was eventually certified. The result was that the nickel was slanting in the esophagus, the food pipe.

The immediate question was how to apply a non-surgical procedure to remove the foreign body. The hospital's physicians led by Dr. Maurice, the medical director, got into a strategy session. In the team were two surgeons and an internist. More than an hour went by; there was no solution in sight. Perhaps in exasperation, the medical director, who was also the chief surgeon, suggested a referral to the John F. Kennedy Medical Center in Monrovia. That would provide an opportunity for evaluation and possible surgical intervention by the thoracic surgeon.

Martha, the little boy's mother, became teary. How could a poor rural woman like her transport both herself and the boy? With whom would she lodge while she attended hospital with the boy? Who would pay for any resultant surgery? The possible confusion stirring her in the eye seemed to torment her. Could she lose her little boy to a single nickel?

In came Mabel! She had long graduated from my alma mater, the Winifred J. Harley United Methodist School of Nursing. She was initially employed by the hospital as a staff nurse, later promoted to a supervisory position. She was known as the Central Supply Room supervisor. And then, she went on to be Scrub Nurse, and Coordinator of the Operating Room. She was also a clinical instructor for OR techniques.

Mabel called the other physicians' attention to what she thought was obtaining. She observed that the nickel was not in the airway as evidenced by the absence of breathing difficulty, and also confirmed by results of the x-rays. Then, she suggested that the nickel could easily be removed with the use of a small foley catheter. They would find whatever direct cavity through the nose until they found a way between the windpipe and the food pipe and bypassed the coin. Fully satisfied that they bypassed the coin, they would gently inflate a miniature balloon attached to the catheter and then pull it up gently. It was clear that Mabel was using her knowledge of anatomy and physiology, especially of the gastrointestinal and respiratory systems. The following image may give a quick sense of what was unfolding.

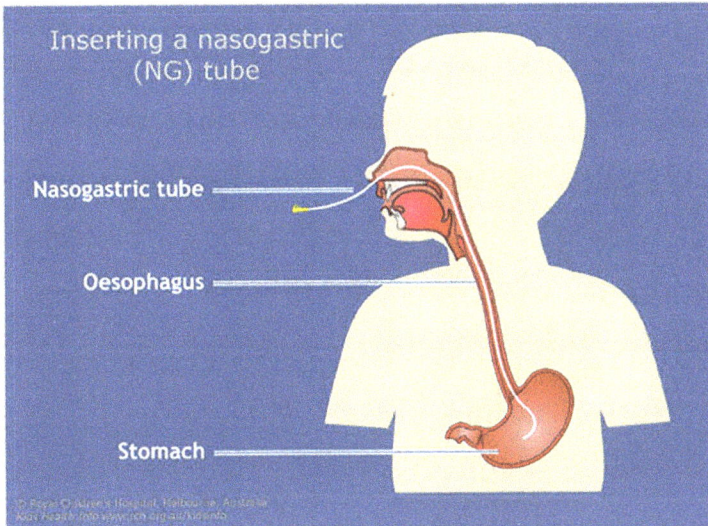

Image of the use of an NG tube

At the back of our throats, there are two pipes—the esophagus and the trachea. The esophagus takes food and fluids down into our stomach while the trachea takes in only air into our lungs. Even a very tiny grain of food going into the lungs accidentally will cause coughing until the particle comes out. There is a structure called the epiglottis that closes the top of the trachea. The epiglottis is like a lid so that when one swallows, what is swallowed doesn't go into the trachea, and down into the lungs.

The medical director was a little wary of Mabel's suggestion. He still maintained that the patient be sent to JFK for evaluation and management by the thoracic surgeon. However, another doctor in the team thought it probably would not hurt to try out the Mabel's suggestion. After a short debate and another review of the x-ray result, they all agreed. They stood by and observed Mabel as she began to implement the procedure which she had laid out. The child was placed on his side as the procedure took off. Several minutes later, their ears were drawn to a mild clinking sound. It was the nickel! It had been ferried up with the catheter through the boy's mouth and hit the back of his front teeth. Mabel immediately but very carefully swept the boy's mouth with her finger, bringing out the nickel. Just then, Dr. Webba, one of the doctors, exclaimed: "Mabel's idea!"

CHAPTER FIVE

Truth Has More Layers than One

Fred the Multitasker and the Stolen Steel Safe

IN THE MID 1980'S I worked in a rural community. There was also a church school. A young adult worked as a Mission boy at the parish house. Actually, he often multitasked between the school campus and the parish house. Both were about half a mile apart. At the school he served as a janitor, doing his chores at the end of each school day. Being a Mission boy and a janitor, he thrived like any other self-supporting young adult. This young man's brother was a junior cleric at the parish. Let's call them Fred and Samuel—Fred, the multitasker, and Samuel, the junior cleric.

In addition to the school run by the church, it ran a reputable clinic. With that clinic I was employed in 1983. I served as a staff nurse, later promoted to a charge nurse. On a short-term basis, I served as a manager. This usually ran for four weeks at a time. It was often in the last two weeks of the year and the first two weeks of the following year when the Mission sisters at the clinic left for their annual retreat in a selected satellite city in the country, or the nation's capital city, Monrovia.

Sometime later, Fred, the young multitasker, was relieved of his employment. He wasn't working either at the school or at the Mission house anymore . He was replaced by two young men, Peter and Andrew. Both attended the church school and, unlike Fred, they were permitted to live in the boys' quarters of the Mission house. Fred had often commuted daily from his parents' home, where he lived.

On one fateful Pentecost Sunday, news broke out that someone effortlessly broke into the Mission house while the Mission administrators were at a church service. The assumed culprit absconded with the pyx, which is the special container in which Holy Eucharist is taken to the sick/disabled if they are absent from service. Not only the pyx. The culprit also sped off with a heavy duty steel safe. This was a safe kept in the Mission house, embedded in a wall. Here funds collected from the clinic, from the school, and from the church were deposited and then later taken to Monrovia for final deposit. Those were days when Monrovia was the end point of major financial transactions.

Only inside helping hands would have known where the steel safe was kept. On this fateful Sunday, when the Mission administrators returned home from service, they met the house entrance unlocked. They knew it was impossible because they reportedly had locked the doors. At about this time, the clear absence of Peter and Andrew from the compound heightened the suspicion. Just where were they! Could they have gone to visit Fred?

A police escort was invited and dispatched. First, the police visited the boys' home. No luck. They went to Fred's home. There they found both boys and Fred playing cards.

After they were found, the decision was that all three would be apprehended and released individually only upon proved innocence. At the police station all three men were questioned by the police. Each denied any knowledge of the crime. Nonetheless, they were detained for further questioning; this time, their parents would be brought in. Now, from the grapevine, it was learned that the safe contained several thousand dollars—some in American currency and others in Liberian dollars. Given the rumored amount, it was no surprise when on the next day, Monday, the school was closed until further notice. After all, without operating funds, there would not be funds to pay teachers and sundry staff.

In solidarity, the church clinic was closed until further notice. On Tuesday, the second full day of the police investigation, Peter and Andrew were released from the police station. An eyewitness had intimated that Fred alone it was, carting away what seemed the steel safe. Carrying it atop of his head through nearby rows of rubber trees had not thwarted any suspicion, as the eyewitness reported. Fred denied an encounter with the witness.

On the third day, Wednesday, local officials decided that they needed some military men to make the clinic staff return to work immediately and attend to the sick people and pregnant women. It should be remembered that Liberia was in the third year of a military coup which had been carried out in April 1980. I'm talking about the coup in which William Tolbert, the incumbent Liberian leader at the time, was assassinated. In such a military era, people throughout the country had to know what they were doing. Any misstep would lead to terrible consequences—fines, imprisonment, or some combination. The officials in the community, many of whom were either military or paramilitary, had initially planned to threaten the local staff. We heard about the plan while people gathered around the police station. This gathering was routinely done from the onset of the thievery. Mary, one of my colleagues, and I met. She was the wife of a prominent official in the town. I told her that putting nurses under duress to treat sick people was a formula for serious medical errors and could lead to fatal consequences. Mary agreed and relayed the suggestion to her husband. The husband worked to bring the threat under control. The clinic and the school remained closed.

Two Boys with a Mysterious Tale

ON DAY FOUR, THURSDAY afternoon, while many people gathered around, anxious to know where the investigation would lead or end, two boys, also students at the school, came to me and my colleagues from the clinic. They came with what at the time seemed a bizarre piece of information. They said they were often commuting to school from a faraway home. They wished school days were over, so they would go ahead to other things in life. Because the incident was really an embarrassment and a point of terrible frustration, they took things upon themselves to consult a local witchdoctor, our version of a shaman. This fetish priest told them that Fred indeed was the culprit. The old man said that people needed to perform certain rituals and the spell with which Fred held the relevant evidence would be broken.

"Time is of essence!" the boys said. "Who can we give this information to act?"

This, as anyone can imagine, was too strange to be true. How really did these boys come by such information? We asked.

Well, someone had overheard their anxious moaning over the closure of school. This person directed them to the old fetish priest in a nearby village. Upon their arrival, they met this old man lying on a mat near a fireplace. He had withered away by a prolonged bout of leprosy. They introduced themselves. In their attempt to explain their mission, he said, "Don't bother. I know why you are here. How much do you have?"

"Two dollars in coins," they replied.

He then gave a drinking cup to one of them to fetch water from a nearby creek.

"Fill the cup with the water and bring it to me. Once you scoop the water, do not look back when you leave the creek."

The old man gave a dollar to the other boy and instructed him to buy a Schnapp bottle filled with cane juice, a locally produced gin, and bring it to him—the old man. The boy did as he was instructed. Afterwards, the old fetish priest dropped the remaining one-dollar coin into the cup of water and stirred in some cane juice. He seemed to see something appear on the surface of the water. It was an image—the image of Fred, the presumed culprit. Thereupon, he told the boys that Fred was steeped in mysticism. The very Fred, said the old man, had ordered a ring for one of his little toes; the ring came from India. This ring often invested him with powers of invisibility. These powers often enabled him to rob from huge stores/business centers with impunity. He stole the money from the Mission house, emptied all contents of the safe into a sack and buried it under a huge tree. Should nothing apparently come of the case, he would dig up the sack and take flight.

"Because of the strong powers Fred possesses," said the old man, "I need time to prepare myself, to wrought myself in the best way possible. I need a few days in order to help me make the ring visible on Fred's small toe."

The two boys had me and my colleagues transfixed. Just what bizarre tale were these fellows talking about that sounded like a fairy tale? Here, we had been submerged in nothing but scientificness. Beyond anything smelled, felt, touched, tasted, seen, or heard, how could any other thing called truth or fact be available? The spin between disbelief and belief was getting torturous.

"Time is of essence," emphasized the old man, and the two boys sailed with the warning voice. "If action is not taken the soonest, Fred will escape from the police cell, and nobody will see him again."

The two boys pleaded with the old man to work very fast, so that Fred did not escape. The man balked. "A one-day emergency ritual is too short. It means suicide for me. If I complete this in only a day, I will die within a week."

Nevertheless, it seemed the old man was over-come with a sense of human suffering. Students out of school, self-supporting students short on resources and craving to complete high school and move on with life, patients left unattended, and diverse sicknesses threatening a serious impact seemed a huge affair worth halting and a situation worth dying for.

He gave the two fellows a substance to rub over their eyes as soon as they arrived at the police station. This would make the ring around Fred's little toe visible and lead to the order of having it removed. With that done, he would be com-manded to go to dig up the sack with the theft items. Stunned by all we were being fed, I suggested that these boys got the police involved. I told them to convince the police to go with them to ascertain much of what they'd told us. They wanted to get the Mission administrators involved. My gut reaction was to argue that because the case was already in the hands of the police, going to the Mission administrators did not really matter. Was something in the back of my mind tugging at me to leave out these white clerics, so that they didn't bring out some element of doubt? Was belief right there and then conquering disbelief? I couldn't really say. Whatever took hold of me did. I probably simply wanted the clerics out of it, period.

The boys agreed and went with the police to see the old man. True to what they had said, the old man also instructed the police officers on what to do. They returned and followed the instructions, saw the ring on Fred's toe, removed it, and then asked: "Where did you bury the money?"

Hollowed meek, he simply said, "Let's go." At about 4pm, the police officers took off in a double cabin pickup, with Fred sitting in the back of the pickup. Speculations regarding the trend of the case floated about the huge gathering at the station. For others, Fred was being taken to the county head-quarters. For others, Fred was taking the police to his home to get the money. For others—well the speculations were growing with all their absurdi-ties. My colleagues and I had the juicy truth. To be privy to a truth or a fact is to feel refreshed and buoyed. But here, we remained tightlipped.

In less than an hour following the departure of the police and Fred, dark clouds literally began to crawl across the skies. Thunder like huge scissors began to rip the skies. Rain burst through it all. We would learn later that curtains to the drama in the skies were rolling back just about the time the exca-vation of the sack began. Eventually, the police got hold of the money along with whatever parapher-nalia, drove to the police station, and threw Fred back into the cell. From there, they headed to the Mission house with the money. Already, another crowd had converged on the Mission compound. The police gave the money to the administrators, or so it seemed. Later, it turned out that the amount reported was not the same amount on record. Howbeit, within twenty-four hours following the recovery of the money, Fred was released upon the direction of the Mission administrators.

And the Old Man Died!

SHORTLY, FOUR OF US nurses from the clinic went to see the local mystic who had helped unravel the stunning case. We arrived and met him lying down by his fireplace under a little makeshift hut. He offered us seats and said: "I know why you are here—to know if the boy acted alone." After a short pause, he said, "Yes, he acted alone. But I'm not going to be around anytime longer. I was not fully prepared before exposing him. The point is that if I didn't act fast, he would've disappeared without a trace. I did the work, but the police gave me only a bag of rice and $25.00. It's ok. The boy will disgrace them soon, anyway."

Few days later, we were reliably informed that the grand theft had not been Fred's first act. Three acts had predated it—one was an encounter in the principal's office; another was a deposit in an old oven. And then how about the theft of a briefcase! Prior to his termination from his Mission boy duties—that is, when he was working as a multi-tasker between the school and the church—a cleric who was a Mission handyman once found USD $300.00 in an unused oven in the kitchen. That day, he was looking for a few old metal pieces to complete some work. Instead of removing the money, he decided to leave it in place and simply monitor how it would disappear. The whole while, he decided to monitor the movement of Fred whom he suspected.

At last, it was time for Fred to go home for the day. The Mission handyman kept watching Fred surreptitiously, but the young man kept pacing the kitchen floor close by the old oven. Half an hour went by. Meantime, the handyman sat by comfortably in a chair at a little table with some materials. He pretended to be busy. Fred would not leave. At last, the man asked: "Fred, do you need help with anything? It's getting late for you to go home." Fred realized that the man would not be leaving the kitchen anytime soon. So, he reluctantly said goodbye and left. That incident obviously alerted the Mission administrators to the fact that Fred was capable of unsightly behaviors. After all, there had been an earlier act—one that occurred in the principal's office.

It had been noticed that as a janitor he was often pilfering money from a drawer of the principal's office and money from stationary sales. The principal's office was always locked. But it was soon discovered that Fred seemed to enter this office mysteriously. So, one day, the oversight Mission administrator decided to lock herself up in the office. It was a quiet plan. As usual, Fred stayed on campus, waited for everyone to leave, and then he started his cleaning chore for the evening. The principal waited quietly and patiently.

To her shock, she later saw the soles and then the toes of an unknown person creeping in, sliding under an adjoining door. The movement was occurring through a center door between the teachers' lounge and the principal's office. The teachers' lounge was always left unlocked for cleaning while the central door and the principal's main entrance were always locked.

Gradually, the belly of the person emerged, then the chest, then the neck, and then the chin came through—under the door! The principal got frightened and almost screamed but she restrained herself as much as possible. Finally, both faces met each other. The startle was palpable. Well, the thief was revealed and suspended, but then he was later expelled from the school when the $300.00 was found in the oven.

Yet, there was another episode of his weaseling that would land him the drama of his grand theft on that fateful Sunday. That episode was prior to his termination as the multitasker. Once the Mission administrator in charge of finances went to Monrovia to retrieve funds for employees' salaries. He returned one evening, and Fred was at hand to assist him offload the vehicle in use. There were several pieces of luggage including a money-filled briefcase, and numerous bags of nonperishable groceries. The briefcase disappeared. The administrator thought he might have left it in Monrovia. He placed a call by radio, but he was informed that the briefcase wasn't there. Not satisfied, he returned to Monrovia. In the end, the loss was assigned to "bad debt." Another money was withdrawn and institutional life continued. It would be long after the Sunday incident that minds would awaken to the possibility that Fred must have taken the briefcase. Anyway, while the administrator was out there trying to find the brief-case, Fred duplicated the house key. Thus, when he was later kicked out of the Mission, he now had a copy of the key, granting him easy access into the house, leading to the Sunday theft.

Such was the trail of "Magic Fred"!

But let us return to the grand theft case. Several days after he was released from the police cell, he traveled down to Monrovia, hired a lawyer, and filed a lawsuit against the police officers who had released him. He charged them with theft, assert-ing that he saw two of them take away money —"huge sums". He exempted the one police offi-cer who advised against taking some of the money. The accused were found guilty and dishonorably disrobed.

And the old fetish man? Barely a week after the discovery of the money, he died—his prediction hadn't been a gimmick!

CHAPTER SIX

We Nearly Lost Her

My Encounter with Gloria

IN 1987, NOVEMBER, I TRAVELED TO some eastern part of rural Liberia to pick up a shipment. The roads from my part of rural Liberia to the eastern shores were very deplorable to the extent that a few hours' trip took more than a day. By late evening we arrived at midpoint of the journey. The driver advised that we spent the night in the city where we had arrived. Here, I knew a cousin and her family lived somewhere in the area, but I didn't have the address and hadn't seen her nor spoken to her in a decade. I asked around and fortunately met a woman who claimed she worked in the school where Gloria was teaching.

The woman "Oretha" escorted me to Gloria's house. I was happy to meet her and her children. It was a great reunion. We (Gloria and I) spent most of the night in my room (the guest room) talking. She did most of the talking, sounded, and seemed like she had waited and wished for a day she would pour out all that was going on in her life, from the onset of her marriage up to how things now were about "the first man she ever knew."

It was past midnight, and her husband was still out. She had mentioned during the chat that it was the newfound habit of his to keep out of the home for hours on end. He had apparently taken delight in openly cheating on her to a point that his women would walk into her home and rain insults on her. They would brag about what he often did for them and did with them. They would describe his genitals, his romantic styles, and every other drama that went with their encounters. That way, they believed she would have no shred of doubt that he did really sleep with them.

Gloria apparently loved her husband so much. She said she often cried every night missing him. His absence from home was killing her, she said. He usually came home when he wanted to. Whenever she approached him on the matter, he'd abuse her—verbally, emotionally, psychologically, or even physically. He was never sorry for his actions. As a result, she started isolating herself, staying away from work because she was not "feeling well." Of course, she was broken and could not perform her duties proficiently. She explained that each time she stepped out, she felt some sense of nakedness. Her sense was that other women seeing her husband's nakedness was a disgrace to her. After all, she felt that he was a part of her, just as she was a part of him.

Gloria complained of health problems. She complained about having "open mole, severe headaches, insomnia, nightmares, etc." Gloria was clearly a very broken woman.

About a year following this 1987 meeting, Gloria visited me at my Cuttington home. During this visit, she told me that she and her family had moved to Monrovia. She complained at length about her husband's chronic infidelity. She also spoke of signs and symptoms of the open mole. I saw all that as part of a classic case of anxiety driven by numerous instances of domestic issues. I encouraged her to see a medical doctor. She agreed. On the second day of her visit, I took her to the Phebe Hospital for consultation. She was diagnosed with anxiety and depression and was provided the prescribed treatment. She followed up with the doctor after a week, as was suggested. Two days after the follow up, Gloria returned to Monrovia. She was instructed to continue her medications and follow up with her doctor in Monrovia. She agreed.

Later, I visited Monrovia and found out that Gloria and the children lived with the husband in their family home. However, he continued to travel out of town as his job seemed to require. Of course, Gloria still believed he was still cheating on her. She and her in-laws were also having lots of feuds. That way, she became very unhappy. About a year later, l learned that Gloria was mentally ill and was roaming the streets. It hit me very hard. I made a few trips back to Monrovia but was never lucky to meet her. And then, my family and I eventually moved to Monrovia to stay.

Few months later, while on my way to work one day, I decided to walk because I didn't have my ride. At a distance, I saw a group of neighborhood children throwing stones at someone sitting in the fence of a Catholic parish. The person was covered from head to toe with a sheet of cloth. I chided the children to stop the stoning, because the person being stoned could get seriously hurt. One or two of the children indifferent to my plea shouted: "That's crazy woman."

"Just stop it. No crazy person deserves to be stoned. This could be someone's sister or mother. Would you like someone to throw stones at your mother?"

"No!"

So, I encouraged them to go away. They left. I continued to my workplace. I don't know what kept my mind lingering on the unknown woman that the children were stoning. Could they return? I really was worried that the children would return to continue stoning her.

On my way from work, I saw the woman outside of the fence of the same Catholic parish that

I'd passed earlier. She was standing against a light pole by a booth. She kept the same cloth covering her. This time, she had the cloth hanging about her shoulders, down to her waist. It was after 5pm. Out of curiosity, I moved slowly towards her. To my great consternation, it was Gloria I was looking at! She was very unkempt. Her body was strewn with open wounds, with the lower legs taking a greater quantity. I called her by name. She simply glanced at me quickly; there was no other response. I introduced myself and asked about her husband. No response. I paused briefly and then asked about her children. At this point I noticed tears in her eyes. She began to sob. I asked if she needed something to eat. She was generous with her yeses. I purchased a loaf of bread with butter and a bottle of Fanta from the nearby booth. She wolfed down the food. "Thank you. This is the first food since today," she said.

As she and I chatted, some neighbors came around. I even noticed some of the children who had stoned her earlier in the day. Many were surprised that I knew her. They said she had paid visits in the area. I had no ear for them. I was focused on my Gloria. I stood there with her for some time.

As it started to get dark, it was also getting cold. It began to drizzle, a strong wind picking up as well. I asked her to follow me home; I lived about two blocks away from the church. She won't budge. In any case, I reached home and got her a blouse and a sweater because she wore only a skirt and the cloth around her shoulders. I asked the gateman at the church to let her into the fence to sleep in the meeting hall and I would return in the morning to take her to a doctor. He hesitated. The parish priest, he said, had warned not to let her or any other person inside the fence. I pleaded with him and gave him a tip. Imagine what money does! He agreed because he said he knew me. Really! Well, I was present when he allowed her in. I promised to pick her up very early around 6:30am. He said that was a good idea. I discussed with my husband that night, including plans to take her to a psychiatrist. He was supportive.

In the morning, fortunately my ride was ready for a workshop. I arrived at the parish as promised. The gateman had just escorted her outside. As it turned out, I convinced her to follow me home. But when we got there, she refused to enter the house to get a shower. "No," she said. "I have maggots on my skin. I don't want to bring them inside." I offered her a chair on the front porch. She sat down. I went in and got her breakfast. She refused to eat. "The food has poison in it," she said. I could not convince her to eat; her mind seemed made up. That reaction, again, broke my heart.

When the car which was to take us arrived, we got on board. I sat with Gloria in the back. We were now on our way to a hospital for psych consultation. We got there. She was evaluated, admitted, and managed at the psychiatry wing of the John F. Kennedy Medical Center. On the day of her admission, the assigned doctor advised family counselling and therapy to provide help and guidance needed to face up to whatever subsequent challenges. That way, she would meet her therapeutic goals while in the hospital and after her discharge from the hospital. With that in mind, I met with her very close family members and her in-laws in their various homes. I asked if they could help. Only her elder sister Susan cooperated. She became the primary caregiver after Gloria's discharge from the hospital.

Sadly, while an inpatient, Gloria had resented her siblings visiting her because, according to her, they never cared for her. They abandoned her in the streets. Obviously, she became very upset that I told them that she was in the hospital. The first day when Susan, her sister, visited, Gloria repeatedly told me, "They abandoned me." She referred to her brother's interaction with her while she was in the streets: "He would pass by me, then give money to a bystander saying give this money to that crazy woman."

Well, Gloria was eventually discharged from the hospital. She stayed with Susan. For three months, I took her to her follow up appointments. Gradually, she became more stable and would go independently. The decision notwithstanding, I often went along to provide whatever additional supervision she needed. As directed by her physician, I continued visiting her home and dressing the wounds on her lower legs. Gloria later moved into her own place. First, it was into a one-bedroom where tools and building materials were being kept. Her children were completing an unfinished family home nearby.

The children and her sister Susan remained very supportive. As said much earlier, Gloria was by profession an elementary school teacher. She applied for a teaching job close to home and was employed. She performed her duties diligently. Later, responding to her children's request, Gloria retired to cater to her grandkids. So ran the life of a sweet soul who would have perished undeservedly under the weight of crippling domestic misfortune. Now, she is a stay-home grandma, watching over her tender ones, perhaps wondering what her life would have been, had other warm hearts and minds not reassured and worked with her, whispering that life has numerous rooms. If one room is uncontainable, another has the capacity for tremendous joy.

CHAPTER SEVEN

Trapped...Almost Without Returning!

IT WAS ONE DAY WHEN WE decided on a health mobile trip to a little village in rural Liberia. I was there as the Registered Nurse/Mobile Health Unit Coordinator. There was a visiting health educator from another part of rural Liberia. There was a nurse aide and a registrar. Of course, there was an ambulance driver for the trip. Our mission was threefold—vaccinate, provide health education, and treat sick ones that would be available. We got through. However, our return trip became something next to the impossible.

We had left home around 8:30am and arrived in the village at about 12:30pm. About four hours got us out there. Like many other places in rural

Africa, getting around is often a challenge. That trip of about four hours could have been simply an hour. A priest who had made several trips out there in every one or two weeks to serve Holy Eucharist told of the terrible conditions of the road. To prepare for our trip, we took along a cutlass or machete, just in case there was the need to clear off tall grass and stubborn vines that would get in the way owing to infrequent use of the path in that rural part of the country.

The road condition was indeed terribly bad. We drove on logs laid in some sections of the road, which were extremely muddy. There was a river with strong rushing waters. The water so crested, it was hitting the bridge. The situation was frightening. We felt insecure because it was clear that in any case we could be swept off if we were not careful. Meantime, tree branches and vines stretching across the road kept flying into our faces. It was so frustrating until at one point I let out a scream: "O Lord!"

"Amen!" another team member said. "This is a good reminder of the whips Christ received for our redemption. This is just a little—all towards helping to save the lives of the less privileged."

She really set us reflecting a lot in the ambulance. We were not deterred. We eventually arrived. Upon arrival, we met one of the priests in the area. He was in the compound of the town chief where the villagers had gathered under a palaver hut for church service. Our team was offered the parlor of the chief's home to serve as the temporary treatment center. We almost immediately went to work. We served the villagers free of charge as part of the goodwill program policy of the Church.

After we were done for the day, we said our goodbyes and boarded our ambulance. The priest we had met joined us because his double cabin pickup had developed a mechanical problem. The idea was that he would get to a nearby town to find a mechanic who would work on the pickup the next day. There was no luck. No sooner had we boarded the ambulance than we saw the fuel light flickering. This was surprising because the gas gauge was at half tank, the amount of which could still get us into town.

Nor could we call into town. Our walkie-talkie had a problem. The battery of the communication gadget ran out. It had given us fading signals earlier in the day. We failed to pay any mind. How complacency sometimes bites deeply! It became obvious that we had no other means of returning home. Almost immediately, the residents got into action. They brought in food for dinner, and the chief provided a sleeping place.

Our current plight at the time was becoming a little more unsettling for me. I was also a fresh mother in three-month nursing. Of course, my baby was on supplementary feeding-formula. Yet, for the worse reaching the worst, my breasts needed some comfort; they were by now experiencing engorgement and discomfort. The mechanical problem seemingly unsolved, we decided to pass the night.

At about midnight, we heard a knock on the front door of the house where we were lodged. We did everything to spring from what was really no deep sleep. Our thinking was that someone might have, on a hunch, come by to rescue us. There was no luck. We opened the door only to see a mother along with other family members come in with a health scare. Their eleven-month-old son was burning with high fever; he was convulsing. The mother said that was the boy's first experience. We got to work to both control the convulsion and to reduce the fever. The treatment ran for about an hour. And when we thought the child was coming through, we found more medications for the mother to take along to ensure that the little boy recovered. The family thanked us and left.

By two o'clock in the morning, we heard another knock on the door. Oh, no—another patient? At last, it was different. A rescue team now arrived from home. Curiosity brought them over. They had been wondering what had happened. They came with a van. They got there all right. But it turned out that their van ran out of fuel. Our long delay had got them so confused that they didn't think about fueling the van appropriately. They waited so long in town, went to the Mission house, and when there was no information to go on, they simply took off, hoping they would meet us on our way homewards. Wrong calculation. At this point, the pickup that needed a mechanic was still around. It did have some fuel. All we did, then, was to transfer its fuel into the van. When the transfer was done, we boarded the van and took off. In about two and a half hours, we returned home. It was a very rough ride home. It was tiring. No dodging or clearing branches or vines. Home was the only pressing thing on our minds.

About a month later, the little boy who had been treated for fever was brought to our clinic. This time, he was suffering from a bout of loose bowels. It had started three days prior to that visit. The parents brought along a rooster for the Mobile Clinic Team. It was, they said, a token of their appreciation for the treatment given during our previous visit. We simply thanked them and explained that given our program policy, we did not accept gifts of any kind from either patients or patients' families. So ended the story. But for a very long time, none of us on the Mobile Clinic Team would ever forget the day when we were trapped and almost did not return home.

CHAPTER EIGHT

When Care Leaves Health Wards

THE CHARLES CASE

IN THE HEALTH INDUSTRY, SOMETIMES THERE is no shortage of errors—both reckless and, sometimes, unintentional. In developing countries medical lawsuits are rare, first because of fewer lawyers trained in medical jurisprudence and second because of poverty to hire these lawyers. And then, again, people dread the pursuing of lawsuits for fear of becoming blacklisted in countries where hospitals and clinics are very few. Sometime ago, there was a reckless error I would never forget.

It was about Charles. He had been medically unstable. It was unsafe for him to be discharged from the hospital where, as an inpatient, he had been undergoing treatment. A protracted hypertensive patient, Charles continued to suffer the ailment until it resulted in a stroke.

His condition grew serious while he was in the hospital. It was difficult for him to swallow food or any related substance. Therefore, a nasogastric tube—a thin, long flexible tube—was inserted through the nose. The tube was lowered into the stomach to get nutrition and medications into the patient. Whatever may have led to a later decision, Charles was discharged while he had the NG tube. Without the guarantee of a Home Healthcare Service personnel, this man going home with the tube was a simply lethal decision. It takes trained personnel to verify an NG tube placement before use and as needed to prevent complications that may become fatal. At home, the man's wife and other family members in the home realized that he was undergoing much discomfort. Thus, out of ignorance, and without the thought of further healthcare consultation, they pulled out the tube. Needless to say, it is only a trained healthcare personnel who removes such a tube when it is no longer needed, or when it is discomforting.

In the end, Charles lost his life at home, not having benefited from post inpatient care.

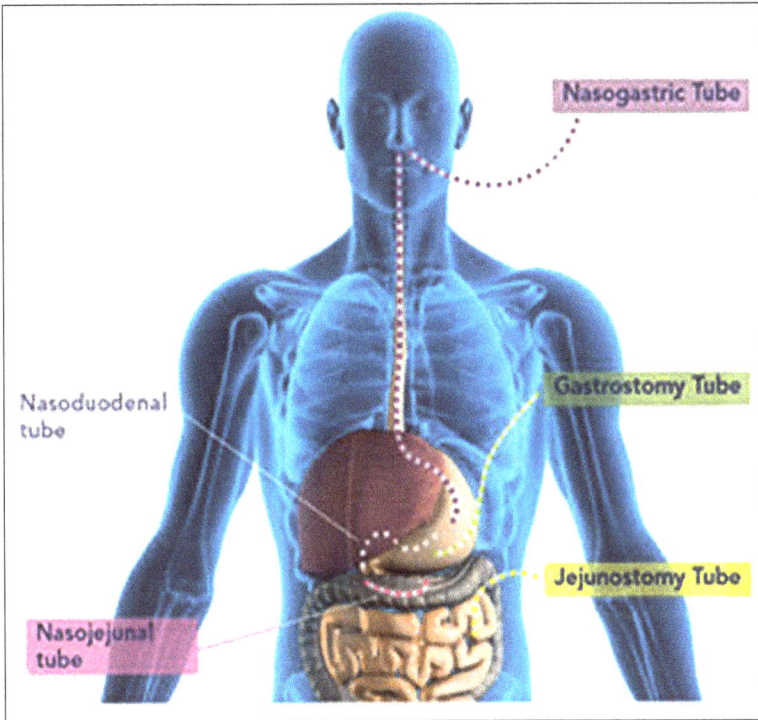

Image of the path of the Nasogastric tube (NG tube).

NO AND JUST NO!
—A MOTHER'S PLEA UNHEEDED

BUT THAT'S NOT ALL the incidents of reckless errors that to this day have affected me. I'll give you one more. It was about a nurse known by a friend. This nurse was admitted at a reputable hospital. She underwent a C-section, an abbreviation of a caesarean section performed often when it appears that the potential mother is incapable of naturally birthing her child, either because she cannot withstand the pain of pushing the baby or because of sudden health complications.

At the hospital, there was a disagreeable woman who happened to be the surgeon. Where professionals are few, patients rarely can afford options. When the nurse's moment arrived, it was determined that a C-section would be performed. The procedure seemed to have gone well. Yet, several weeks later, the woman began to feel severe discomfort. It turned out that she was carrying a foreign object as a result of the surgery. Her initial inquiry was rebuffed. After several rounds of quiet inquiry, she learned through a whistleblower that surely an object had been left inside of her.

Nevertheless, the surgeon remained adamant—she was definitely sure all objects had been removed. No other effort to the contrary was entertained. How about an x-ray to ascertain the possibility? Nope! A possible out of court settlement might be acceptable. Nope!

THE MOTHER'S CASE
...THE NEXT TIME AROUND

LIKE MANY SUCH CASES, that woman's plight has remained haunting. What could have been possibly done? I understand that each case possibly has several facets to it. But research shows that the human body is very delicate; therefore, any hands and minds coming to it need to be alert at an optimum level. Perhaps, the following thoughts are worth considering.

Objects Most Commonly Left Inside the Body After Surgery

Leaving foreign objects in a patient's body is a mistake that may be avoided if extra safety precautions are taken. As a student nurse at W. J. Harley practicing at the Ganta United Methodist Hospital, I had opportunities to witness several surgeries of different categories during the study in operation room (OR) techniques. Depending on the type of surgery, as varied health writings and studies will always confirm, the types of surgical objects commonly left inadvertently inside a patient include:

- Sponges
- Scalpels
- Scissors
- Towels
- Drain tips
- Needles
- Guide wires
- Clamps
- Twisters
- Forceps
- Scopes
- Surgical masks
- Measuring devices
- Surgical gloves
- Tubes

The most common objects left inside a patient are needles and sponges. Sponges in particular are difficult to keep track of. The reason is that they are used to soak up blood during surgery and tend to blend in with the patient's organs and tissues. These incidents happen most during abdominal surgery, and that region is one of the most common areas where surgical objects are left inside a patient.

Why Objects Get Left Behind

Surgical objects are unintentionally left inside a patient for a number of reasons. Hospitals typically rely on nurses or technicians to keep track of the number of sponges and other surgical tools used during surgery. Human errors come into play as incorrect counts can be made due to fatigue or chaos as a result of a surgical emergency. Furthermore, several factors can increase the risk that an object may be left behind after surgery. These factors include unexpected changes that occur during surgery, multiple procedures that may be needed, procedures that may involve more than one surgical team, and procedures that may involve greater blood loss.

The Errors, the Impacts

The consequences of surgical tools or objects being left inside a patient's body vary from harmless to fatal. Sponges and other surgical implements can lead to infection, severe pain, digestive system problems, fever, swelling, internal bleeding, damage to internal organs, obstructions, loss of part of an internal organ, prolonged hospital stays, additional surgery to remove the object or even death, and so on.

So, Then, What to Do?

Surgical sponges make up the vast majority of objects left behind after surgery. During my early life of nursing, manual sponge count before surgery and before closure of the top layer of the patient's surgical spot was mandatory. It had to be implemented by the surgical assistants (the scrub nurse and the circulating nurse) in addition to their specified duties. From research, I've learned that in developed countries there are various types of sponge tracking technologies now available to ensure that foreign items are detected and not left inside the patient, and that adopting sponge-tracking technology has also proven to be more cost effective for hospitals than having to perform additional surgeries to remove unwanted surgical objects.

My final note is one repeat that should never hurt at all: caution, caution, and more caution will go a long way in reducing surgical death rates, grave surgical complications, and prolonged and costly litigations.

CHOICY?
...GOT TO BE CAREFUL!

ONE OF THE THINGS I've noticed in life, and perhaps this is not all too unique to me and only me, is that even though providing options to patients or customers is a brilliant idea, if the patients or customers have not built the capacity to choose well, another problem may be generated—rejecting what could be very beneficial. To choose a productive option depends on developing a toolkit of questions. Finding a health professional that is very competent to serve should be foremost to all other reasons for accepting a service or the caregiver.

In the next story to talk about, a rural woman was interested in engaging with a doctor who, for a frivolous reason, did not seem a doctor until her life crawled on line.

Black Hands No Touch; White Hands, Yes!

That was while I was a W. J. Harley student. I was doing my OB/GYN practicum at the Ganta United Methodist Hospital where black and white doctors worked together. As a student nurse, I was assigned in the OPD (Outpatient Dept-prenatal clinic). In prenatal care, "a pregnant woman receives health care from an obstetrician or a midwife. Services needed include dietary and lifestyle advice, weighing to ensure proper weight gain, and examining the woman for any related maternal problems of pregnancy."

It came the turn of Kou Tokpa, a woman who was in her last trimester. The OB/GYN care team positioned her for monitoring. She presented a transverse lie, meaning that the baby was lying sideways across the tommy inside of the mother rather than being in a head down position. During Kou's visit, she was taken into the screening room, vital signs checked, and she was made comfortable by the nurse aide while she waited for the physician to come in and see her.

A few minutes later, the physician, we'll call him Dr. Wilmot, entered. Just before he could start the assessment process, the patient muttered: "I want to see the *kwi plu.*" She suggested that she wanted a white doctor to attend to her. But the white doctor she was referencing was on a short vacation. He had traveled to Monrovia, the nation's capital city. Reassured he heard Kou well, Dr. Wilmot picked up his medical implements and left the room. Kou, too, left and went home without being seen by the physician on duty.

It seemed that Kou did not return to the clinic again until it was time to give birth. One night, her family rushed her to the labor room. She was in labor; her condition was critical. Now, the physician on call was Dr. Wilmot, the very physician that was on duty during her last prenatal visit. The midwife on duty that night placed a call to the physician. It seemed Kou needed to undergo C-section. The midwife had simply said that there was a patient in grave need—the patient had come in with an abnormal presentation, making normal delivery very impossible. The physician rushed over. Suddenly, he realized that it was the same woman several weeks earlier. "I'm sorry," he said to the staff. "I can't work on this patient. Until my skin turns white, I can't work on her, let alone perform a C-section." With that, he walked out of the room. The staff on duty that night were very astonished hearing that from a physician, and considering the current situation of the mother and her unborn child. None in the staff knew the back story.

As hours passed, the fetus was noted to be in distress, the mother was getting exhausted, the staff kept calling and pleading with the physician without success. The midwife in-charge called the chief surgeon, an Egyptian, and updated him. Africans from north Africa look white. He spoke with the on-call physician, but the on-call physician maintained that he could not help her unless his skin turned to a white man's skin. He gave the details regarding his decision and his permission to another doctor to perform the surgery. The doctor agreed but pleaded for the presence of the on-call doctor in the OR during the procedure. Dr. Wilmot, the on-call physician, agreed but said he would not be assisting.

About a day after the procedure, Dr. Wilmot made his rounds and at Kou's bedside, he told the available staff what had transpired several weeks earlier. And then said, "I did not want to aggravate the situation. Without confidence in me and perhaps her fear of reprisal, anything could have gone wrong—even fatal."

Kou became all apologies.

The power of storytelling is that one story is told and before the storyteller realizes it, several flashpoints spring about here and there. As I sometimes reflect on this part of my experiences, I can only think about a certain psychiatrist of the French Caribbean World. I'm talking about Frantz Fanon. I'd heard about him and the book he did many years ago. In that book, *Black Face, White Masks*, he spoke about how the White World has conditioned the Black World to often think less of itself.

Now, I understand that racial matters are sensitive, since on one level throwing broad statements around is somehow unsettling. For me, like many others who grew up in parts of the world different from America, the white and black experience have been a little different. In my day out there, our part of the world was populated by American Peace Corps. It also had been populated by Catholic nuns and priests. It had been populated by white missionaries from other denominations and religions. Most of these people had been phenomenal in engaging with us. The gut feeling about black and white relationship, therefore, is to see whites more as human beings than to see their color and hastily condemn them as a group. After all, they too saw us and treated us more as human beings. The point is that those in my category as I've been describing would rather treat this black and white relationship on a case-by-case basis.

But considering Fanon, I get it. One needs simply to respect the man's observations on the matter of race relations. Fanon's focus on race relations was driven by events of history—slavery, colonization, etc. History, as it is well-known, rarely stays silent on such matters. Perhaps keeping such themes on the front burner has a major social benefit. In the current era of inequities in the distribution of health and other social amenities in even the developed world, it is a serious point that we all should be prepared to keep the related conversation alive. That way, hearts and minds will be awakened to do a lot of soul-searching and, in the end, do positive things to make the world a warm and very sweet place to be.

Anyway, Fanon made it one of his missions in life to urge black people of the world to believe in themselves, to apply knowledge and skills in ways to improve themselves in this sometimes racially charged world. If only one would have a voice to speak in the words of Rodney King who pleaded in a tense time, despite the brutal beating he got from the police in Los Angeles: "Can we get along?" Perhaps, if all races of the world saw more good than bad in each other and made it a mission to teach the lesson of respect, love, and the beauty of working together without disrespect, without condescension, it would be so affectionate a world. We do need such a radiant world today!

DEATH MARCH TO HALT

The Scare of a Tubal Pregnancy

AND HOW CAN I forget two more connected stories that emphasize the role of the trained health

practitioner in a community! One of the stories occurred in the late 1980s, shortly before the
Liberian civil war. The other occurred in the early
1990s when the war was experiencing its stretches of
slows. This meant that, at one time several months
on end, the fighting would rage. And then all factions
would be called to some African capital for a conference. After that, there would be some break, only
for some dissatisfied faction to spring into action
over some alleged violation by another faction. The
restlessness that comes with such wartime phenomenon is never anything to wish upon anybody, not
even on an enemy. After all, long stretches of cer-
tainty drive planning for the future. If uncertainty
pervades the land, how do schools operate? How do
children attend school and study effectively? How
are financial forecasts done? How do the employed
obtain their paychecks to pay bills?

In any case, it was, first, the late 1980s, shortly
before the Liberian civil war. A woman was brought
to the hospital at which I was working. That was
in rural Liberia. She came in complaining about
some abdominal pain. It seemed that she was in
the early stages of pregnancy. It turned out that she

was experiencing tubal pregnancy, but that was not initially detected. To understand a few things about tubal pregnancy, you, perhaps as a lay person, need to understand a few basic things about the reproductive system. This is all about the parts of a woman, and a man, that need to work together to produce a baby. For the woman, there needs to be four basic things—the female genitalia, the cervix, the uterus, and the fallopian tubes (one on the left side, the other on the right side). For the man, it's the male genitalia.

When the woman and the man mate, the man produces a substance known as the sperm. The sperm count is often in the millions. But the miracle is that usually just one makes it into the region of the female eggs (ovaries). And equally, out of millions of eggs, it is usually only one that meets the sperm. At appropriate, specific times, the sperm meets the woman's ovum or egg cell. It is a relatively long journey. You may understand why it takes nine whole months for a child to form and be born.

First, the sperm must move from the female genitalia, cross the border called the cervix into the uterus or the womb. Then it turns up to one the fallopian tube. Much friction has to take place. The sperm continues until it finally meets the woman's ovum at the end of that tube. Some other friction has to take place producing a special ball of cells (i.e., the fertilized egg) that is now ready to roll through the tube down to the uterus or the womb, where the sperm had earlier passed. In the uterus is where all the transformation that leads to the formation of a real human being will take place.

If this ball of cells is too big for the tube, it will hitch on the way. Stuck, it begins to expand right there. Think of a piece of dough, which is the size of a marble expanding to the size of two or three of that marble. That hitching accident creates what is called the tubal pregnancy. Since the presumed pregnancy occurs outside of the womb, there is a scientific term for it. It is called ectopic pregnancy. There are few other types under ectopic pregnancy—i.e., pregnancy outside of the womb—like the tubal pregnancy, but for now the focus is on the type which, we now know, is the tubal pregnancy.

It is almost like someone trying to swallow something and it hitches down the throat with no easy way of getting it out, except through surgery. The ball of cells in the specific fallopian tube expands to the point of causing the mother great discomfort. The incident is like pregnancy, but as you may now imagine, it is not real pregnancy. If it is not detected and operated on, the ball of cells may rupture, and excessive bleeding may even put the woman's life in serious danger.

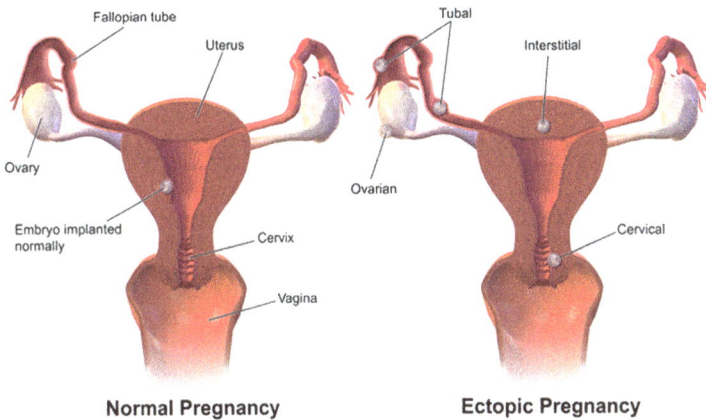

Comparative images of normal pregnancy and tubal pregnancy

Through my training, experience, and constant review of health literature, I came to know that tubal pregnancy would often occur through a number of things, including instances of hormonal imbalances, the abnormal development of the ball of cells (i.e., the fertilized egg) formed during the meeting of the ovum and the sperm, a woman getting pregnant even though she underwent tubal ligation, or the presence of a scar tissue. Serious impact of sexually transmitted diseases may also lead to tubal pregnancy.

Tubal pregnancy is really one of several deceptive ailments somewhat difficult to track. It often starts off seemingly as a normal pregnancy. When it starts, a woman misses her time. Her breasts feel very tender with slight engorgement. She every so often feels nausea. If tested for pregnancy, it turns out positive. Yet, incidences like light virginal bleeding, the pelvic and abdominal regions as well as the tips of the shoulders feeling much discomfort, etc. may be quick reminders to probe a little more.

I should say right here that what I briefly outlined about the reproductive system and the incident of tubal pregnancy is just a mere tip of the iceberg. There is often a lot more information to walk through.

Anyway, in those days of the late 1980s, the woman came to the hospital. The doctor I was working with did not catch the problem. Nor could I, not on his level of training, raise a voice. Of course, such accidents do occur. No doubt, that is why health teams are very important. But they tend to spring into action when cases get a little more serious.

I went home that day after my shift. However, I remained somewhat troubled. I went about my chores, including shopping for the home. But I remained restive. On my way from shopping, I went to the woman's home; it was in the evening. The woman was the wife of a man who often sewed my clothes. When I got to the house, the man had gone to get a taxi to take her to a nearby village. The couple wanted to try out alternative medicine—the use of herbs, roots, etc. I have to say that in developing countries, numerous minds tend to run easily and quickly to that type of medicine, first, because for people, especially in the rural parts of the countries, it is an aspect of a cultural predisposition and, second, because it seems to be the cheapest form of health treatment.

When I got to the house, the woman was lying down helpless. I ran a quick test. It wasn't long when the husband returned with the taxi. I told them there was a serious complication that herbs could not treat. We had to return to the hospital, I said. They cooperated.

We got to the hospital and went straight for the emergency room. It turned out that the tubal pregnancy had ruptured. The doctor and staff went into action. The case that would have turned fatal was reversed. Obviously, sometime later we were all relieved.

Hepatitis Strikes

NEXT WAS THE HEALTH case of the 1990s. Here, I should begin by saying that one of the troubling aspects of concepts related to attitudes and behavioral change is the question of perception. Someone who either has grown up with a certain way of thinking or has learned a certain way of doing things cannot easily unthink the thought or unlearn the certain way of doing things. Of course, the thing about perceptions in cultures does not have anything to do with whether one is talking about developing or developed countries. It has to do with human beings everywhere. For example, what is obtaining in even the United States of America remains an eye-opener. I'm talking about the thousands or even millions of anti-vaccination campaigners or deniers of Covid-19 who have created conspiratorial theories. And how many have not died from such conspiratorial theories! In any situation like this, relentless health education and patient reassurance can be useful antidotes. Better still, the next point cannot be easily contested: "Experience is the best teacher of all times."

It was in the early 1990s. The civil war was going through its intermittent breaks. By then I was in Danane, the Ivory Coast. In the community that my family and I lived as refugees, the couple whose wife had been treated for tubal pregnancy in the late 1980s became our accidental neighbors. As for that, perhaps there should not be any incident in a person's life that is really called an accident.

Over time, the man became sick. One day, I saw him. His eyes were deeply yellowish. His skin grew even darker. It turned out that he had hepatitis. This disease attacks the liver and weakens functions of the kidneys and related organs. When the right medication is not found, trouble appears. Immediately, I advised the wife to take him to hospital. They brushed off the advice. They mouthed the often repeated denial. Hepatitis, locally called "yellow jaundice," had no cure in Western medical treatment—according to them. Herbs, roots, and exotic soup, including soup with the meat of a snake of the boa constrictor species, were often prescribed by fetish priests.

The days went by. One day, a neighbor went to fetch food for the day, saw one of the prescribed snakes, bought it, and brought it to the family of the ailing man. Joy had no bounds. The wife cut up the snake and prepared soup for him. He drank the soup and was very happy for the most part of the afternoon, playing and dancing to music. Sometime later, the joy and the energy he seemed to carry began to fade. The reality was that the soup had no effect. Meantime, a pills peddler, something common in developing countries, kept bringing around pills—paracetamol and the like. Very harmful, very unproductive! Many of such peddlers were not trained. They simply were in it for a mere trading activity. Most of them sold over-the-counter drugs. Even when these people sold more potent drugs, they rarely knew the side effects of those drugs, or drug combinations.

One day, I went to visit the home. I found the man, my tailor, very weak and helpless. I also met in there a pills peddler. I told him to just leave. Right there and then, I told the sick man's wife to get the man to hospital as soon as possible. Now the couple's anxiety piqued. The wife sent word to her brother who was in transport trade to come over at once to help them transport her husband to a hospital in rural Liberia. Shortly, the brother arrived, and both were transported to Liberia.

They arrived at the hospital, all right. But the staff out there were disappointed that the wife had kept the man for so long a time, instead of bringing him in sometime earlier. With little or no treatment in twenty-four hours, the man's brother-in-law in Monrovia was contacted. He traveled to the hospital immediately. Soon, they were on their way to Monrovia, the Liberian capital. The man was admitted at the St. Joseph's Catholic Hospital. Here, they found the long craved cure. Here, they found the much sought mental relief.

It has been many years now. The couple continues to thrive in Liberia, West Africa. We recently reconnected. It was a beautiful and refreshing phone chat. "Your life still beats in us!" the man quipped. "It's God. It's God," I chimed softly.

CHAPTER NINE

A Reunion Unlike Any Other

Ms. Loretta Gruver, Please....

IN MARCH OF 2010, I TRAVELED from
Columbus, Ohio, to Ashville, North Carolina. I
traveled on a Greyhound bus to visit Ms. Loretta
Gruver, the retired nurse educator. She was a hero,
my hero. As you will remember, she had taught me
at the Winifred J. Harley United Methodist School
of Nursing. Having worked in Liberia all those long
years up to the Liberian civil war, she returned to
her home country, the United States of America.
She lived at the Brooks-Howell Home, which is
a retirement home for Methodist missionaries. I
arrived there at about 9am. At the reception desk,

I was accorded a very warm welcome. I signed in and stated the purpose of my visit. The receptionist asked if I planned to pass the night. That way, a room would be prepared for me. "Thanks," I said. "I intend to stay until 6pm and then leave."

"Oh, ok., then. I'll take you to Ms. Loretta's room."

When I got to her room door, her caregiver was just about to wheel her out to the spa. I was offered a seat close to her room until she got ready. Her caregiver then asked me to join them. I assisted with her transfer from her wheelchair into her recliner where she was made comfortable. She recognized me, although she had begun to develop speech impairment. I could tell that she was now physically challenged. *Life!* I thought. She asked about my husband; I told her that he was at the moment in Liberia.

As we chatted, I looked about her room. On the walls, she hung maps of landscapes of parts of rural Liberia, where she had served. She also showcased handicrafts of the leprosy colony with which she had served.

Time seemed to fly by. Lunch time came around. The receptionist would not allow me to go far out for lunch. She told me to use the cafeteria of the retirement home facility, free of charge. I thought that was an impressive gesture. After a very sumptuous meal, I returned to Loretta's room. We talked for a little more time.

Two hours to my departure, I updated her about efforts of the Winifred J. Harley alums to establish the Winifred J. Harley U. M. School of Nursing Alumni Association in the Americas, an idea I initiated in 2008. I told her that I was the interim chair, but that elections for permanent officials were pending. That was not all. I listed several names that made up the group.

"We intend to hold a Hill House style of festivities," I said. No need to explain further. She still remembered Hill House festivities which often came as a prelude to annual graduation. Fun at those festivities was often out of the world. Oh, past school life! The name of Hill House festivities seemed to stir something in her; a grin crossed her face. Just then, I also shared with her a letter which one of the past students wrote for the efforts to begin work on the association. Here it is below:

Thanks to you Mrs. Franklin. This is a noble resumption of our quest for unity among the graduates of the famous Ganta U.M. School of Nursing (i.e., Winifred J. Harley U.M. School of Nursing). Some of us consider ourselves very blessed to belong to this group. I never try to imagine what life would be like without Ganta. It is a unique way to realize that the past influences the present, because without what was, nothing is. I also want to thank others who have made some attempts in the past to unite us. I am sure that with renewed energy, we will make some progress. Success = persistency.

Oh, how happy I was for that visit in March 2010! Little did I know that I was there to give Ms. Loretta Marie Gruver her flowers while she was alive. My professor, my friend, departed these human shores on May 5, 2010. Many others and I continue to owe a lot to this wonderful woman. Loretta left her beautiful home in the United States and went on a missionary journey to Africa! It was early in 1964 when she took that journey and was stationed in Gompa City,

Nimba County, at the Ganta United Methodist Hospital.

Who would forget her! She and her colleagues trained nearly 200 competitive Liberian nurses. Yes, she also taught at the Winifred J. Harley United Methodist School of Nursing, where she served as the Director of Nursing. She held that position until the Liberian civil war spread death and destruction all over the land. Besides professional knowledge and skills, she infused her students with values of sincerity and honesty. The competency, the care, and the deportment demonstrated by alums from W. J. Harley spoke highly of this tireless soul's dedication to duty.

Anyone who passed through those W. J. Harley walls had to celebrate Ms. Gruver's memory! I do celebrate her. I am very proud to have been a product of her professional creation.

And why won't I! During the chaotic days of April 1980, the time of the military coup in Liberia, Ms. Gruver became an anchor, a pillar of strength. Some of us were freshmen then. Her embassy, the American embassy, advised all Americans to leave the country for their own safety. But this strong woman assured us that as long as the W. J. Harley walls were still standing and she had life, she was not going anywhere!

Ms. Loretta M. Gruver kept her word with us—we who were depressed, thinking we were about to lose an important opportunity for an education, a nursing education! She took us through the highs and lows of life. By this singular dauntlessness, she became our Joan of Arc! And now in a different role and place, here she's become our Angel! "What we are is God's gift to us. What we've become is our gift to God."

Oh, to be in the midst of numerous other alums! Oh, to stand among them and raise and sing with perfect delight Ms. Gruver's favorite hymn: "This Is My Father's World."

And how about those yellow papers!—often a signal for pop quizzes. Hmm—now we can think it's fun to mention those yellow papers! In those days, our muscles would grow tight! Our brains almost freezing—pop quizzes! Today, we can think about the yellow papers in fond ways. Little did we know, or care to know, the path of mental and emotional preparedness to which you were directing us, Ms. Gruver!

Today, I use yellow papers as part of my ID. See what life is? Sometimes our pain becomes our joy the moment we understand how things work together for our common good. Thank you, Dear Teacher: Many years gone! But it is as if it were just yesterday when we were your students, when you would come, racing to our dorm rooms for inspection. Funny enough, instead of creeping in, you'd come knocking loudly, "Inspection time, inspection time!" Were you evil, you would have simply sneaked up on us and flogged us numb. But there was the love in your heart for us. And later the Super Senior hour, which was a part of the graduation season, would come, and we'd gather at the Hill House, a house ancient and often cleaned for the hour, for pre-graduation festivities, exchanging pleasantries and bathing in love.

Mortal life may have robbed you away, but never, never will we ever forget you. Our Mentor, our Teacher, Our Inspiration, Our All!

CODA

LOOKING BACK ON ALL I'VE EXPERIENCED as a professional nurse, I have drawn a rewarding, personal culture from the nursing profession. I have developed a lifestyle driven by a sense of commitment; a sense of integrity; and a sense of industry, meaning, the urge to always work very hard. So, I have grown into a person of Commitment, Integrity, Unflinching Determination, Patience, and Tolerance.

My Guided Tools

PATIENT QUALITY CARE, SAFETY, and Satisfaction are the tools that have made me the kind of Nurse I am today. Such tools have given me the ability to work with patients, patient families, staff under my direct supervision, my colleagues, and with others from various cultures without fear, doubt, or favor, no matter what their ideas are about me at first sight or as human connection continues in our various assigned areas of work. I DO NOT FORGET MY TOOLS. They have molded me into a very calm and patient Nurse even under *Critical Care* circumstances. Keeping consistently focused on my tools has neither proved me wrong nor undesirable in my pursuit of the purpose of Nursing Care.

Finally, I don't intend to be presumptuous. However, should any aspiring Nurse or a professional colleague need a word from me, I would safely say the following: I believe every Nurse understands the purpose of this Noble Profession, from the prescribed training days to the day of practicing Nursing. Does this profession match the person's passion? Since the individual's initiation, has some personal comfort been achieved? Has this professional spot proved the right spot? If this specific Nurse is finding it challenging to follow Florence, I intend to say forthrightly: "You had rather Submit, Learn, Commit, or Simply Quit!"

It is never too late to learn to use the right tools, lining up the real purpose of this profession. Also, it is never too late to quit if you know that you are in Nursing for the wrong purpose. Tell yourself the truth: "I really do not belong here. I must leave and enter into what I can do best with all my heart, mind, and soul for the best reward, both to those I serve and myself."

www.ingramcontent.com/pod-product-compliance
Lightning Source LLC
Chambersburg PA
CBHW060317100426
42812CB00003B/808